January 2

Venice,

D0867297

THE LAW OF LOVE

The Law of Love

Ann Beals

The Bookmark
Santa Clarita, California

Library of Congress Control Number: 2003103950

Beals, Ann.
The law of love / by Ann Beals.
p. cm.
ISBN 0-930227-45-X

1. Spiritual healing. 2. Christian Science. 3.
Jesus Christ--Teachings. 4. Love--Biblical teaching.
5. Prayer--Christianity. I. Title.

BX6943.B43 2003   289.5
    QBI33

Published by
The Bookmark
Post Office Box 801143
Santa Clarita, California 91380

CONTENTS

INTRODUCTION

The subject of love is as old as time and as universal as the air we breathe. Yet, do we really understand it? What is Love? If Love is Principle, as Christian Science teaches, then Love is a law, and this law should be given long and serious consideration, for obedience to this law is the only way out of mortality. Through Love, we find the kingdom of God within. Therefore we should ask ourselves, Do we know *why* we must obey this law of Love, and how to do so?

I first began searching for the true meaning of spiritual love many years ago. I read an article on Christian Science entitled, "Nothing Less than Love." In it was this profound and challenging statement: "It is a spiritual and scientific fact that no matter what happens, no matter what anyone says, no matter what anyone does to us, we are never justified in expressing anything less than Love, divine Love. We must never want to do anything to anyone other than to bless him."

When I read this, I thought, "Is this possible — never to express anything but love?" At the time I seemed to have relationships that were anything but loving. Often things were said and done that I felt were terribly unjust, unloving and undeserved. I didn't imagine these wrongs; and because they seemed so real and so personal, resentment, anger and hurt feelings would well up and take control of my thinking. Although humanly I may have been justified in reacting as I did, I knew from this statement that I was violating the law of Love. I was also the one who suffered from this disobedience. When I reacted emotionally to these wrongs, I was not happy, things went wrong, the conflict was magnified and prolonged, sometimes resulting in a physical problem. Always in some way I suffered from my own unloving thoughts. And I suffered until I stopped thinking them. When I learned to forgive and forget, I stopped suffering. It was that simple.

Through these painful experiences, I began to grasp the profound significance of the fact that we *must* love. We have no choice but to work at unselfed love until we actually demonstrate it towards everyone, everywhere, all the time — regardless of what they say or do. We must love all that our thoughts rest upon. Love has to be the medium we live in effortlessly.

Simply to tell others that they must love is futile. The reasons for doing so must also be explained. Lofty platitudes and absolute statements about the divine Principle, Love, are worthless unless we know how to go about demonstrating this Principle, and spiritual love becomes a law to our life.

Those who live the law of Love are very rare indeed. Occasionally we meet individuals who have no hate or selfishness within. They radiate an atmosphere of gentle love combined with wisdom, strength, patience and forgiveness. Yet it seems that humanity as a whole finds living unselfed love to be the ultimate challenge. With the abundance of good that man has accomplished during the last century alone, it seems strange that peace and plenty are not becoming a reality for the whole of humanity. Slowly we are coming to realize that too often the greatest accomplishments leave untouched the selfishness, hate and fear in human consciousness that shut us out of the spiritual good we long to have. The mortal elements that generate the meanness, grossness, and coldness of a materialistic world remain to be destroyed. Only as humanity understands why it must obey this law and does so, will it rise above the darkness and chaos of mortality into the glorious freedom that spiritual love alone can give man.

The purpose of this book is to explore the law of Love in the light of Christian Science, and to encourage you, dear Reader, to master the mortal elements within, transcend even human goodness, intellect and affection, and demonstrate the unselfed love that will open up for you God's kingdom within. Obedience to the law of Love will bless you beyond anything you can imagine.

Somewhere in time, the collective effort of world thought to demonstrate the law of Love will outweigh the antichrist; and when this takes place, we will begin to see, as John did, a "new heaven and a new earth" coming about as concrete reality.

Ann Beals
2003

Chapter I

THE LAW OF LOVE

And when these things begin to come to pass,
then look up, and lift up your heads: for your
redemption draweth nigh.

CHRIST JESUS

We live in the age of Love's divine adventure
to be All-in-all.

MARY BAKER EDDY

Civilization is in the throes of a mighty evolution. A spiritual age is dawning. The times are both thrilling and frightening, for the foundations of yesterday's world are crumbling beneath us, and a clear vision into the future has not yet come into focus. It is not the end of civilization, but the end of a material form of life as we have known it.

Human organizations — government and business, education and economics, religion and medicine, marriage and family — are in a state of traumatic change. Scientific discoveries have blessed humanity with awesome wonders; but the age-old problems of crime, disease, drugs, and war are unresolved; and technology continues to create new problems while solving old ones. Human resources are proving inadequate for coping with a multitude of challenges that the individual faces each day. It would seem as though a spiritual vacuum is spreading through the world, sinking it deeper and deeper into the darkness of materialism, humanism, and scientific technology, all of which continue to create an ever greater estrangement between God and the human mind.

1

In the complexities of modern life, the individual is being swept along by the forces shaping his world — forces over which he often has little or no control.

Yet for those seeking a way out of this turmoil and confusion, there is an answer. Through a *transcending intelligence*, we can triumph over the challenges of the present times. Over two thousand years ago, Christ Jesus revealed this way of escape when he said quite simply, "The kingdom of God is within you." He also said that no one is excluded from this heavenly kingdom; all must eventually find their way into it.

Through a better understanding of the spiritual nature of God, man and the universe, we can transcend the present form of intelligence and develop a new concept of creation. This new knowledge will enable us to be in control of our life.

The Law of Love Defined by Christ Jesus

This advanced intelligence is based on God as the only cause and creator. The idea of a divine origin to the universe and man can be traced as far back as earliest Bible days, when Abraham first discerned one God, spiritual and eternal. Throughout the Old Testament, the presence and power of one God was taught by Moses and the Prophets. They furnished many examples of man's ability to control evil and matter through a spiritual understanding of God.

This spiritual power culminated in the healing works of Christ Jesus, who provided evidence of the dominion that God has given man over all things, a dominion that is found within the hidden realm of Love. Christ Jesus possessed this transcending intelligence in such depth that he could overcome the entire illusion of matter and evil, and prove them unreal. His healing works were not mystical, but the result of an advanced intelligence that he considered to be natural to man. By healing sin and disease, raising the dead, walking on the water, and multiplying the loaves and fishes,

2

he proved the truth he taught. He illustrated the power for good latent in the realm of Love.

Jesus' obedience to the law of Love enabled him to overcome death itself. He passed through the crucifixion and emerged from the tomb triumphant over matter and mortality, proving for all time that a spiritual understanding of God is the way out of the mortal dream.

During his ministry, Christ Jesus alluded to the spiritual enlightenment that would come with the promised Comforter. Although he left the complete explanation of his healing works to a future period, his teaching regarding spiritual love was explicit, for love is the key to the spiritual dimension; mankind had to reflect divine Love to some degree before the promised Comforter could be understood and accepted. Jesus taught that God is Love. He stressed compassion, humility, forgiveness, forbearance, honesty, meekness, goodness, loving your enemies, refraining from judging and condemning others. He summed up his teaching in two great commandments: "Thou shalt love the Lord thy God with all thy heart, and with all thy soul, and with all thy mind;" and, "Thou shalt love thy neighbor as thyself."

Following his ascension, his followers spread the gospel of Love which became the heart of Christianity. Paul wrote: "Love is the fulfilling of the law." John instructed the early Christians: "Beloved, let us love one another: for love is of God; and every one that loveth is born of God, and knoweth God. He that loveth not knoweth not God; for God is love."

During the Dark Ages, Christianity spread over Europe, uniting Western civilization in one fundamental religion. God became known as a rational Father, which led to the idea that He must have created a rational, or scientific, universe — one that could be understood. In the beginning of the scientific age, the first scientists were seeking to understand God through an understanding of His creation.

3

The Coming of the Promised Comforter

As millions of Christians lived this religion of love, and the Age of Reason replaced old theology and superstition, there came about a mental climate that was gentle and enlightened enough to accept the teachings of the promised Comforter. Into this warm and intelligent atmosphere, Mary Baker Eddy fulfilled prophecy in 1866 with her discovery of Christian Science. She introduced the revolutionary idea that God is the universal divine Principle, Love — an absolute law to man's being.

With the discovery of Christian Science, the teachings of Christ Jesus were transformed from a religious philosophy of Love to a practical Science of Love. The idea of God as the rational Father of the universe evolved into God as the *divine Principle* of the universe. In this way, Christian Science replaced the belief in a man-like God with a well-defined, scientific Principle. For the first time the spiritual and scientific laws underlying Christ Jesus' healing works could be understood and proven universally.

In the Christian Science textbook, *Science and Health with Key to the Scriptures*, Mrs. Eddy explains the spiritual nature of God and man, and the unreality of matter and evil, including sin, disease and death. Her discovery accurately defines the qualities, laws, energies, structure and contents of the spiritual realm. It establishes the healing works of Christianity on scientific laws.

Although Christian Science was discovered over a century ago, it is still little understood, and the healing power latent in the spiritual realm has barely been tapped. Even with the purest of motives and the most dedicated effort given to understanding God, few have even faintly approached the spiritual healing works of the Master Christian or the Discoverer of Christian Science.

And so the question remains, How do we enter this kingdom that waits within the inmost thoughts? How do we achieve dominion over matter and mortality, and escape from the discord and confusion of these latter days?

A New Vision

In Proverbs, we read, "Where there is no vision, the people perish." It would be a dark time, indeed, if there were no vision into the spiritual dimension. But God has graciously provided us with a vision of such depth and scope, that we can begin here and now to know and live in this realm of Love. We enter this invisible dimension through an understanding of Christian Science. Seen in relationship to the overall scientific picture, *Christian Science is a scientific discovery of incredible magnitude.* In this century, the physical sciences have gradually pressed through the visible universe into a nonmaterial realm underlying the universe — a realm that is generally considered to be the origin or cause of creation.

In spite of the progress made by the physical sciences, this hidden realm remains a mystery because its nature is not material or mental, but spiritual. To understand its spiritual nature, the mind must be permeated with some degree of spiritual love, for the nonmaterial dimension discovered by physics and the hidden realm that Jesus called the kingdom of God, are one and the same. The time has come when science and religion are beginning to meet and merge into one harmonious system of ideas, and Christian Science is the first bridge between the two.

Mrs. Eddy writes in *Miscellaneous Writings* of "the line, plane, space, and fourth dimension of Spirit." This fourth dimension is not a dimension conveniently invented to explain phenomena that the physical sciences can't explain. The spiritual dimension has always existed. In entering it, we are simply becoming conscious of a universal Mind outside of, and beyond, our own. We are developing a mental depth that is new to human consciousness.

Understanding God scientifically as the cause of creation, is the next step in the orderly development of science and religion. As this evolution comes about, the healing works of early Christianity will be understood scientifically and practiced universally.

Christian Science is the first accurate and complete explanation of the hidden realm of Love. It gives form and substance to the "fourth dimension of Spirit." But even with this new Science as a key to divine reality, this hidden dimension does not give up its secrets easily.

If heaven could be reached by brave or super-human deeds, or intellectual brilliance, or magnificent leadership, or creative genius, or religious devotion, we would have reached the millennium long ago. But the prerequisite for understanding divine reality and demonstrating its healing power, is the daily living of the Sermon on the Mount, and this seems to be the single most difficult thing for human nature to achieve.

An Individual Work

The chemicalization throughout the world is forcing us to press on in this challenging work, and explore this spiritual realm of Mind, for this realm alone offers workable answers to present-day problems, and a way to escape them. There has been a great erosion of individual rights and freedom in modern times. As we have grown more and more dependent upon others, we have felt the control over our life slipping away. How often we seem to be at the mercy of conditions, circumstances, relationships that are discordant, and we can find no way out of them. Yet Christ Jesus was independent of all external conditions. *He governed his life subjectively and controlled everything that came into his experience mentally, through the advanced intelligence divinely bestowed upon him.* Because finding the kingdom within is an individual awakening, we have only to use our own mental resources to understand this hidden realm and draw upon its healing power. As we develop divine intelligence, we grow increasingly independent of outside conditions.

We enter the kingdom of God subjectively, through an education in spiritual things. We each emerge into the spiritual realm

6

through our own awakening to the Christ-consciousness within. We must draw upon our own inner resources, and think and pray our way into it. Because this is a subjective experience, no one can obstruct our unfoldment and progress, or influence God against us, or reverse our healing work, or prevent us from entering this holy place. Neither can another do our work for us. Each is required to do his own work, and make his own way. As he does, each reaps the reward he has earned.

Entering the kingdom of God is a long-term commitment. There will never come a time when we are instantaneously transformed by some mystical experience into a conscious awareness of the kingdom within. We enter it *gradually* through phases of spiritual growth. Christian Science reveals an orderly procedure for our emergence into this kingdom. While each individual will experience in his own way a deliverance from evil, the study and practice of Christian Science hasten this transformation of consciousness. We should first become familiar with the letter of Christian Science through consecrated study of the textbook, *Science and Health*, and Mrs. Eddy's other writings. As these are studied in conjunction with the Bible and other works on Christian Science, we gain a thorough education in the letter of Christian Science. We must also understand Christian Science treatment — the prayer of affirmation and denial. The treatment was given by Mrs. Eddy as a scientific form of prayer.

Study and treatment are the means through which we advance in Christian Science. Without these two essentials, Christian Science remains a theory without the healing works that prove we understand it. But once we have learned to pray scientifically, we begin to have healings. As we grow more accomplished in the treatment, we can then press forward into the next phase — *learning the law of Love.*

Step by step God leads us in this challenging adventure into the realization that God is all and evil is nothing. As we accomplish these progressive phases, we discover that we are in the kingdom of God here and now.

An understanding of the divine Principle, Love, is the phase which leads to the kingdom of God within. Let us then give long and serious consideration to learning about God as Love, for this will lead us beyond a rudimental understanding of Christian Science into our God-given dominion over all evil and matter.

The prayer of affirmation and denial is explained in my books, *Animal Magnetism, Scientific Prayer, Christian Science Treatment: the Prayer that Heals,* and *The Prayer of Affirmation and Denial.* The further explanation of the phases we go through in reaching an elementary state of spirituality is found in my work, *The Secret Place: Footsteps to Finding Your Oneness with God.*

Chapter II

LOVE OPENS THE WAY

Strait is the gate, and narrow is the way, which leadeth unto life, and few there be that find it.
CHRIST JESUS

The Divine Being must be reflected by man, — else man is not the image and likeness of the patient, tender, and true, the One "altogether lovely;" but to understand God is the work of eternity, and demands absolute consecration of thought, energy, and desire.
MARY BAKER EDDY

With Christian Science, we have the means for understanding the kingdom within, but its presence as a concrete reality remains hidden until we have demonstrated some degree of spiritual love.

There are many reasons for learning to obey the law of Love. Love is the Christian way of life. Obedience to the Sermon on the Mount is proof of our love for God and man. We also learn in Christian Science that love heals and prevents sickness, disease, discord and adversity. Furthermore, love is a strong defense against aggressive mental suggestion and mental malpractice. But there is another major reason for obeying the law of Love.

The kingdom of God is within; therefore we enter it from within. This experience is entirely *subjective*. It is a mental renovation that takes place through spiritual enlightenment. In the heart of consecrated study and prayer, we realize the unfoldment of spiritual ideas and intuitions. These are "God's thoughts passing to

9

man," as Mrs. Eddy explains in *Science and Health*. Such moments of realization transform the mind. Instead of having faith in God, we begin to understand Him. *Through the unfoldment of spiritual ideas, we enter the kingdom within.*

This transformation of the mind does not take place automatically. It does not come through faith and human goodness. It does not come with time. Neither can we contrive or originate an image of the spiritual realm with the darkened human mind. We cannot bring it to light through rationalization or intellectualism. We cannot force it to unfold. Spiritual ideas that transform the inner self are the *gift of God*. They appear in consciousness as we become receptive to them, and are prepared to understand them. At one time they are not in consciousness, and then they are. At one time we do not know them, and then we do. As these ideas unfold one by one, they spiritualize consciousness. And in this way we think and pray our way into heaven.

It is absolutely essential to realize that *we are entirely dependent upon God for the spiritual ideas that reveal the kingdom of heaven to us.* We must understand that human logic, intellect, opinion, wisdom and rationalization do not reveal the divine facts of being. A spiritual understanding of God and man comes as individual revelation. It is given by God to the receptive thought.

Since we are told that the Father does not withhold any good thing from us, what prevents the unfoldment of these ideas? It is the failure to handle the error or evil claiming to be our own consciousness that violates the law of Love. Animal magnetism, entrenched within, blinds us to the presence of God. *It hardens the heart and soul and mind, and prevents the appearance of God's ideas.* The mind hardened by materialism and sensualism, is impervious to God's thoughts. It cannot hear God's voice speaking to the inner self. To the degree that the mind is buried in mortal traits, emotions, and beliefs, it is opaque, dark, unreachable. So long as our mind is hardened by self-will, fear and hatred in their

10

many obvious and subtle forms, we shut out the spiritual ideas that unfold subjectively and transform consciousness.

Each individual is living in the construction of his own mental universe. Each mind has its own peculiar combination of thoughts and feelings, its own unique identity or personality. At the present time, this identity is mainly formed by the belief in the power and reality of matter and evil, and by the negative traits and emotions that such beliefs produce. There is a basic sameness to this universal mentality. *Many forms of hatred, fear, and selfishness are so common in collective world thought that we never consider them to be wrong.* We may not question these mortal emotions because we do not want to examine the error within our own consciousness. It is the nature of mortal mind to defend and justify itself, to resist change, and block the unfoldment of spiritual ideas.

Because the law of Love is related so strongly to spiritual feelings, demonstrating spiritual love has to do more with emotions than intellect, for it is *mortal emotions* that obstruct most effectively the unfoldment of God's thoughts. How often do we blame others for our problems? refuse to yield up our human opinions? justify the unloving things we say and do? take pride in some of our mortal traits and argue against giving them up — even when we know they are a violation of the law of Love?

Many mortal traits are so universally accepted and practiced, and seem so natural and harmless, that we think in them effortlessly. But in so doing we harden the mind to the unfoldment of God's thoughts. Unless we understand the difference between the mortal and immortal nature of man, we daily violate the law of Love without realizing it. This fact is so basic to our spiritual progress that I cannot emphasize it enough. Spiritual progress begins when our daily work is focused on discerning the animal magnetism within, and reforming the inner self through learning spiritual love. We actually *re-form* the mental structure we think in.

The Three Degrees of Mortal Mind

In *Science and Health* we are given a basic guideline for demonstrating the law of Love. On page 115 is found the "Scientific Translation of Mortal Mind." This translation includes three degrees: the physical, the moral, and the spiritual. The First Degree is the physical, or "Depravity." It shows a total absence of spiritual love. It outlines basic mortal mind: "Evil beliefs, passions and appetites, fear, depraved will, self-justification, pride, envy, deceit, hatred, revenge, sin, sickness, disease, death." This degree specifically defines animal magnetism. Even the most insignificant and seemingly harmless human weakness or sin is, in the last analysis, part of this degree. These are the mortal elements that harden the mind through defying the law of Love.

We may quickly read over this First Degree, assuming that we are beyond this stage. Evil beliefs, depraved will, passions and appetites, hatred, revenge — these would hardly define a consecrated student of Christian Science. But I would not pass over this degree too quickly. It covers many subtle forms of animal magnetism that must be detected and corrected before we can be entirely free of the First Degree.

The Second Degree is the moral, or "Evil Beliefs Disappearing." It gives the transitional qualities: "Humanity, honesty, affection, compassion, hope, faith, meekness, temperance." In this degree, we see the Christ-consciousness appearing, for these qualities are derived from divine Love. This Second Degree transcends mortal emotions. It represents pure, unchanging, unselfed love — kind, gentle, forgiving, patient, understanding. It is the Christ-love defined, and therefore it is a softened state of consciousness that is receptive to spiritual ideas.

In the Second Degree, Mrs. Eddy is reaffirming Christ Jesus' Sermon on the Mount, telling us that the deeper things of God may presently seem mysterious, but the law of Love is some-

thing we can understand and demonstrate here and now. We see
that it has more to do with the emotions than the intellect. The
tender Christ-love precedes the full unfoldment of Truth given in
the Third Degree.

The Third Degree is the spiritual, or "Understanding." It
lists the spiritual qualities of being: "Wisdom, purity, spiritual understanding, spiritual power, love, health, holiness." And how anxious
we are to be in this degree! But as we study these three degrees,
we see that we must go *through* the transitional stage in order to
reach the third and final stage.

I have noticed that some students try to enter the third
stage of spiritual understanding without learning the second stage,
assuming that these qualities are not too important, or that they are
already expressing them. It is tempting to make this unfortunate
assumption, for the qualities of the Second Degree appear on the
surface to be rather simple and undemanding. Perhaps we read
through the Second Degree hastily, thinking, "Yes, yes, I *am*
humane, affectionate, honest, meek. I *am* loving." But too often
we mistake personal goodness and affection for spiritual love. We
can have many good qualities, and still embody so much animal
magnetism that we remain at the First Degree level. Do we really
understand the full meaning of honesty and compassion and meekness and affection?

The demonstration of this transitional stage is an exacting
and demanding spiritual lesson, one we cannot avoid. It is important to realize how challenging it is to demonstrate fully this Second
Degree, and we must learn it *before* we can graduate to the Third
Degree. It is in this Second Degree that we begin to turn the letter
of Christian Science into the spirit. And so we cannot pass over it
assuming that we express these qualities. A superficial treatment
of this stage means that we do not understand its importance, or we
do not want to be obedient to the law of Love. In trying to bypass
it, we are left in the mental darkness of the First Degree. The
advanced understanding of the Third Degree will not unfold until

we have learned unselfed love. If we want to find the kingdom within, we must take the Second Degree very seriously and dedicate ourselves to a thorough demonstration of its requirements. Only then can our power to heal begin to manifest itself on a certain and scientific basis. Only then can we approach the final stage of spiritual development.

Unselfed love is so alien to the mortal disposition that demonstrating the Second Degree is a great challenge for most of us. To master it requires an inner renovation that completely transforms our present mental atmosphere. This degree requires us to leave behind familiar mortal traits, and yield up our most cherished personal thoughts and feelings for an education in spiritual things.

This work is comparable to an education in a specialized vocation or profession. In the study of advanced academics, we consciously mold and develop our mind to be accomplished in a chosen field, such as architecture or engineering or accounting. The knowledge we seek out and acquire actually changes how we think. In like manner, we may also consciously mold and develop our feelings to be loving and forgiving. In Christian Science, we educate our emotions as we educate our minds; we discipline our emotions as we discipline our minds. Thus we have enlightened emotions as well as an enlightened mind. This is the lesson of the Second Degree — to reform our heart and soul and mind to obey the law of Love.

We must work at this until a Christ-like love becomes the natural medium in which we think and live. We must live it in our hearts when we are alone, and in our private lives with those who are close to us, and daily with everyone we come in contact with. There can be no duplicity about this. Spiritual love has to rule from the inmost thoughts to the farthest reaches of our mind.

Perhaps as we read in the Second Degree of compassion, honesty, meekness, temperance, we do not think these qualities are too challenging. But this unique combination of qualities is the most difficult of achievements to master in its entirety.

14

Love as a Spiritual Law

Mrs. Eddy writes of God as the divine Principle, Love — note she writes of the *divine Principle, Love.* Being Principle, Love is a law to man's being. Unless we recognize that Love is a law to man, we will not know when we are violating this law, and to recognize the penalties such disobedience brings.

Let us compare the divine Principle, Love, to the physical laws operating in the universe — laws of gravity, aerodynamics, hydraulics. We must understand and use physical laws intelligently for scientific technology to work properly. These laws are basic building blocks in the structure of the universe. Man did not invent these laws, nor did they suddenly become laws as he discovered them. They have always been laws governing creation. As man became aware of them and learned to use them intelligently, he began to exercise dominion over his environment.

The spiritual realm underlying the visible universe is governed by moral and spiritual laws. Just as physical laws have always governed the visible universe, so spiritual laws have always governed the invisible elements of the universe. They do not become a law to our being as we learn of them. They are ever-present laws that govern us whether we know about them or not.

With the discovery of Christian Science, Mrs. Eddy discerned that there is a spiritual dimension to the universe, which has a clearly defined structure of divine laws in the same way that the physical universe has a structure of physical laws.

In this hidden dimension rest the moral and spiritual laws governing man. These laws are as inviolate as the laws of physics. In time we shall realize that we have no choice but to obey them. One of the first laws that we can understand and practice is the law of Love.

The law of Love is like the law of gravity. When we defy the law of gravity — even though we seem justified in doing so —

15

we suffer in going against it. Even if we had to jump out of a burning plane or we accidently fell off a cliff, the law of gravity is no respecter of persons or circumstances. We pay the penalty for going against it.

Even so, in the spiritual realm, the law of Love is absolute. We cannot ignorantly or willfully disobey it without eventually paying the penalty. Therefore, when we study the divine Principle, Love, we are learning of a spiritual law that is as omnipotent and omnipresent as the law of gravity. Since disobedience to this law shuts us out of the kingdom of God and brings severe penalties, it is imperative that we make it our business to understand it.

We may consider the divine Principle, Love as a perfect way of defining God. But so often we consider spiritual love as far removed from the daily grind, the market place, the trials and tribulations of the mundane life we live. It does not seem a practical requirement to be always loving — as though we had a choice to be or not to be loving. But Christian Science shows that we do not have a choice. Spiritual laws are as absolute and inviolate as physical laws. We have no choice but to obey them.

This work of learning love cannot be superficial or hypocritical. It must be thorough and sincere. As we understand the allness of God and the perfection of man, we will not even *think* or *feel* unloving toward anyone or anything. When the inner self is purified of personal sense and void of hate or fear or selfishness, we are incapable of unloving thoughts.

There are many subtle forms of self-will, hatred and fear latent or active in our thinking. We may not always act in willful or hateful ways. We may not always say angry or critical things. But *what are we thinking?* Are we guarding the hidden thoughts and the secret, silent feelings that occupy our inmost thoughts? We should not only leave unloving things *un*-said and *un*-done, but we should leave them *un*-thought and *un*-felt. This requires that we discipline our emotions to the utmost. To violate the law of Love, we do not have to say or do hateful things. *We only have to think*

16

hateful thoughts, fearful thoughts, selfish thoughts. It all begins with the inner self. And here we come to the root of discord, sickness and disease — thinking and feeling unloving thoughts. *We must refuse to think or feel unloving toward anyone or anything at any time for any reason. Period. No exceptions.* If we refuse to think or feel unloving thoughts, we cannot speak or act in an unloving way. And therefore, we cannot defy the law of Love.

Human Affection or Spiritual Love

When we are told to love, our first reaction is to claim, "But I *am* loving!" However, human sentiment is not the same as spiritual love. Human affection, intellect, and wisdom are not substitutes for spiritual love. Human warmth and goodness are more desirable than a cold, stolid heart, and precede spiritual love. But personal affection is limited to certain persons, places, things. It is changeable. It is easily offended, and can turn to hate, anger, hurt, coldness, self-justification, revenge — sometimes within minutes.

With human affection, all is well so long as we are in the company of those who agree with us. But what happens when we are offended by those who are hateful, immoral, selfish, cruel, dishonest, dominating, deceitful, worldly, materialistic? Then the animal magnetism dormant within comes forth to control us. When we are attacked or victimized by an unloving, unchristian person, we react with criticism, anger, hurt feelings, animosity, disappointment, revenge, unforgiveness.

Human affection can be very strong and yet leave untouched a host of negative emotions that cause us to act or react in violation to the law of Love. Moreover, human goodness and affection do not protect us from sickness, disease, and adversity. When the humanly good person seems to experience sickness and adversity, this is due to the fact that, in spite of his human goodness, *he still fears and believes in the power and reality of evil.* We must face the fact that human goodness alone will not deliver us

17

from evil. Only as we graduate beyond human affection and goodness into spiritual love and understanding, do we begin to escape this false conviction of evil's reality, and the pain and discord it seems to give us.

Yet this transcending step seems so hard to take. When we talk about spiritual love, it seems so simple. But the very act of expressing love to everyone, everywhere, all the time, of thinking and feeling only kindness and forgiveness without a relapse into anything less — this seems to be the single most difficult demand ever placed upon the human mind and heart.

My friend, it often takes superhuman strength to return love for hate; not to make a reality of the abuse and injustice of animal magnetism; not to react to it; to stand in the face of undeserved coldness, indifference, misunderstanding, personal wrongs, and demonstrate such dominion that we do not react with similar emotions. When we do so, when we return quiet patience, forgiveness, kindness, and understanding to those handled by animal magnetism, we are demonstrating spiritual love.

Spiritual love is considered by some to be weak, effeminate, ineffectual — almost powerless in handling evil. But Mrs. Eddy once wrote, "Love is a mighty spiritual force." Through spiritual love alone, we gain dominion over evil. During the time that we are learning to live spiritual love, we must keep before us the fact that we are not trying to impress others or relate to them on their terms. We are proving to God our desire to obey His law. We are also proving to ourselves that in the end we will not lose any good thing by doing so; rather, we will gain entrance to the kingdom within.

At this point in our spiritual development, spiritual love is the single most important thing for us to understand and demonstrate. Following our preliminary work in learning the letter of Science and the treatment, it is our first major spiritual lesson — the one that often separates the earnest student from the believer in Christian Science. The Christ-love that we make our own through study and prayer, can stand unmoved when encountering the most vicious forms of animal magnetism. It never reacts. It can separate the error from the person, and make nothing of the error while forgiving the person. It can face evil and with Paul say, "None of these things move me."

God the Source of All Good

What causes us to be unloving? This question should be carefully considered in order to demonstrate the Second Degree.

Hatred, selfishness, and fear are the result of the belief in the reality and power of evil and matter — a belief that claims to be concrete conviction in the heart of consciousness. We believe that evil — as person, place, or thing, as circumstance or condition — can threaten or destroy or deprive us of the good that we feel is rightfully ours.

We can be very consecrated Christian Scientists, filled with love and faith and good works, but because of the conviction in the reality of evil and matter embedded in mortal consciousness, many forms of hatred, selfishness and fear, remain as part of our human disposition. These mortal traits may not be too apparent so long as our life runs smoothly. But when animal magnetism seems to cause adversity or discord of any kind, the latent mortal traits surface, and we violate the law of Love in expressing forms of hate, selfishness or fear.

As Christian Scientists, we *say* there is no evil or matter, but in our hearts most of us are more convinced of the reality of animal magnetism than of the allness of God. Because of this, we also believe that we are dependent upon matter and mortal mind for everything necessary, good and desirable in our human experience. Fear and hatred often seem to control us when we believe that someone or something is threatening or destroying our health, supply, or relationships.

Without some insight into our oneness with God, good, we continue to believe that others can deprive us of our money or

THE LAW OF LOVE

material things, underpay or overcharge us, cheat or rob us. If not today, then tomorrow. We believe they can take away our good name through gossip or slander, and separate us from those we care about. We think they can rob us of our peace and joy by disappointing or abusing us, defying or deceiving us, offending or ignoring us. We believe that world conditions, accidents, unforeseen events and circumstances, can destroy our health and supply. If we act or react in an unloving way, it is usually because we believe that our good is in jeopardy.

Through the belief in matter or evil, we see our good as coming to us *objectively* — that is, through material means, dependent upon persons or circumstances. To the extent that we depend on matter or persons for our good, we cannot be entirely free of the more aggressive and entrenched mortal traits that harden the mind.

So long as we see our problems as objective — or originating in the outer world — we will not recognize that it is our own conviction in the reality of evil that is the controlling factor in our life.

The main purpose of our study of Christian Science, is to learn that God is all and evil is nothing — and to demonstrate this fact in every avenue of our life. We see in the life of the Master Christian that he was in no way dependent upon persons or circumstances outside his own consciousness. He relied upon God alone for everything. Mrs. Eddy writes in *Unity of Good*, "With Christ, Life was not merely a sense of existence, but a sense of might and ability to subdue material conditions."

Christian Science gives us this same spiritual dominion. Through study and treatment, we learn how to handle animal magnetism, and to prove that our life and all that relates to it is not controlled by evil, but by the divine Principle, Love. The one Father-Mother God supplies our every need. To know this enables us to turn to God for all things. As we prove to ourselves that all good comes from God, the false conviction in the power and reality of evil begins to disappear. With it go the mortal traits that accompany this belief.

Spiritual love must rest upon the understanding of God as the source of all good. Christian Science exposes the unreality, the nothingness, of evil, and enables us to demonstrate the allness of God, good. It makes spiritual love practical. As we study and pray daily, we learn to demonstrate health, supply, relationships, and trust God to care for our daily affairs.

Think about this carefully, for it holds the secret to learning the law of Love. Through our study of Christian Science, we learn that all good comes directly from God to the individual. There is no power greater than God. If He gives you something, it cannot be denied you or taken from you. If He gives it to you, He also supplies the channels needed for its unfoldment. All of your good comes directly from God to you when you have demonstrated it. It is not sifted through any special person or group of persons. You are not dependent on any outside source for a single good thing.

If you have demonstrated any good thing, no one can keep it from you or take it away from you. Nor can anyone influence God against you. God unfolds to you all good. If something comes from God, it must unfold as a concrete reality. If it does not come from Him, it will not bless you, and you do not want it.

The more we prove this, the more secure we are in our trust of God to care for us. We look away from persons to God for the supply of our every need. When we learn to do this, obedience to the law of Love is not difficult.

21

Chapter III

THE FIRST DEGREE
MORTAL TRAITS AND EMOTIONS

*Whatsoever thing from without entereth
into the man, it cannot defile him . . .
that which cometh out of a man, that
defileth the man.*

CHRIST JESUS

*The anatomy of Christian Science
teaches when and how to probe the self-
inflicted wounds of selfishness, malice,
envy, and hate.*

MARY BAKER EDDY

In order to overcome the traits and emotions that darken
the mind and heart, we first need to recognize those that claim to
make up our mortal personality. It is not too difficult to define the
more obvious forms of sin — especially in others. The consecrated student of Christian Science is usually beyond such traits as
depraved will, malice, envy, hate — or so it would seem.

But there are many forms of animal magnetism that handle
us and darken our thought without our realizing it. Many of these
traits are considered normal, or even essential, to one's personality.
They go undetected because we do not realize that they are classified in Christian Science as sin.

We are going to consider now a long list of mortal traits, or
sinful elements, many of which are such universal forms of animal

22

magnetism that we think in them effortlessly. They even appear to be normal or natural. Because those with whom we associate usually have the same general emotions and beliefs that we do, we become accustomed to them and never question them as being ungodlike.

Detecting these mortal traits is essential to our spiritual journey. We may study Christian Science diligently, and have a very good intellectual grasp of it, and still not be able to heal with any certainty, because life-long traits of the First Degree — habitual thought-habits and emotions — remain predominately greater than the Christlike qualities of the Second Degree.

In order to outgrow the First Degree, we should consider how we relate to this list of mortal traits. As we study these various forms of sin, the reader may chemicalize, or become disturbed and agitated over them, for they are so common that we can identify with many of them if we are honest with ourselves. It helps to keep in mind that these false traits are universal. We *all* have them to a greater or lesser degree. If it seems difficult to admit that these forms of animal magnetism are handling you, always remember that these are the elements that harden the mind and seem to separate you from God.

As you consider these traits, please realize that they have never been part of your true identity, and therefore you *can* overcome them. Mrs. Eddy once told a student, "God has ordained for us all good, and He will remove our sins from us as far as east is from the west, when we want to give them up." And so the sooner you recognize these false traits and pray to be delivered from them, the sooner you will enter the kingdom within.

The List of Mortal Traits

The following list has been compiled with my own analysis of each trait in its more obvious form. It is the result of *my* study, but you will want to develop your own insight into them, and consider the more subtle forms through which they may be handling you. You alone can determine which ones you need to overcome.

Personal Sense: Personal sense is the I, the ego, the focal point of mortal mind. Totally absorbed in itself, it is all of the forms of selfishness known to the human mind — self-will, self-justification, self-love, self-righteousness, etc. Personal sense is the term for all the beliefs and emotions of the First Degree that make up a mortal personality.

Personal sense is always concerned with itself, always thinking and saying, "I want . . . I think . . . I have . . . I believe . . . I know . . . I like . . . I hate . . . I am so mad . . . I won't put up with this . . . I am so hurt . . . I can never forgive him . . . I . . . I . . . I . . ." Personal sense can be termed "I" trouble, for the mind is obsessed entirely with one's self. Personal sense is the opposite of spiritual sense. It is only concerned with what it is thinking, saying, doing, its appearance and health, the impression it is making on others. It craves attention, understanding, recognition, approval. The false traits listed in this chapter — and many that are not included — make up the nature of personal sense.

Being totally self-centered, rather than God-centered, personal sense takes everything personally. It is easily offended, even by unintentional and imagined wrongs. It has on-going feuds with those it dislikes, and is often embroiled in arguments and disagreements with those who offend it.

One may think he is beyond personal sense because he considers himself a very good, honest, responsible person. He may assume that, because he is so good, always "doing the right thing," he should not have to endure wrong treatment from others. When he does encounter what he considers to be unkind, unjust, abusive experiences, he reacts with anger, distress, hurt feelings, hostility, vindictiveness — any number of First Degree emotions. This indicates that, for all his human goodness, he still embodies many personal emotions that are latent in consciousness until provoked into action by the animal magnetism in others.

Personal sense personalizes good, making idols or enemies of persons. It gossips, pries, is curious about the affairs of others. It is so immersed in the material world of persons, places, things, that it has little or no rapport with the spiritual world of Truth and Love.

Self-will: All forms of human will are the opposite of God's will. Self-will is the underlying force of mortal personality. It forces, drives, demands, strains, pushes and manipulates to achieve its ends. It can be obstinate, stubborn, uncooperative, unwilling to yield to others. It can also be sly, cunning, clever, even diabolical. Almost every problem we have can be traced to aggressive or thwarted self-will. Mrs. Eddy refers to it in the textbook as "the sensuous reasoning of the human mind." And she also says, "Human will is capable of all evil." Depraved will is determined, aggressive, even ruthless, in getting what it wants.

As a rule when self-will is mentioned, we may quickly assume that we are not guilty of *that*! But in fact, subtle forms of self-will can be the single most challenging false trait to detect and cast out. We work out of self-will by degrees. As we recognize the harmful effects of human will, we learn to give up personal striving and pray, "Thy will be done." This willingness to know and obey God's will softens the inner self, and we yield more readily to His directions.

How can we know if we are using self-will? If there is a sense of pressure, stress, striving, drive, in what we are saying or doing; if our thoughts, words and deeds produce friction, frustration, discord, aggravation, irritation, and a host of other negative emotions in ourselves and others, then we are exercising self-will.

Quite often a good and conscientious person will be imprisoned in his own self-will in that he plans, outlines, creates responsibilities and schedules and long-range plans, and then *forces* himself to live up to them. He may force others to do so. The use of self-will in the name of good is self-deceiving. The zealous but inexperienced and unwise effort to accomplish good through self-will is detrimental to spiritual progress.

Once self-will begins to give out, divine ideas, creative ideas, intelligent ideas, practical ideas, can unfold moment by moment as we need them. Giving up self-will does not leave a vacuum within. It is replaced by God's will unfolding the ideas we need day-by-day. We cannot pray enough to be shown the way out of self-will into obedience to God's will.

Self-planning: Very much akin to self-will is self-planning, which acts through self-will. Planning of some kind is usually necessary to get through the day, but we need to remain so flexible that we can change when we are shown the need to do so. Plans made from selfish motives and acted upon through self-will leave little room for God's plan to unfold. Through personal outlining and planning, the future becomes a fixed obsession in consciousness. Self-planning obstructs God's plan for God directs through the unfoldment of spiritual ideas which move forth into fulfillment. We each have a place in God's plan; each has his own purpose in the universal design of divine Mind. Our work is to pray to know His plan, rather than outlining our own based on selfish and materialistic motives. As we grow spiritually, we plan less and pray more to know God's plan. Mrs. Eddy once wrote of God, "He plans every detail of our affairs." Yielding up hard-core personal planning, softens the inner self and allows God's plan to unfold.

Selfishness, self-love: A selfish mind is concerned exclusively with its own selfish desires, seeking or concentrating on gaining that which is to its own advantage, pleasure, well-being, without regard for others. Selfish thought is entirely motivated by *getting*, never giving. Aggressive, or depraved, self-will can not endure being crossed or denied its way. An extremely selfish person is so concerned with himself that he is insensitive to the discord, distress, pain and mental anguish that he causes others in having his way or getting what he wants.

26

The kingdom of God within, is God-centered, not self-centered. One can begin to overcome the hardened state of selfishness as he learns to give, rather than to get. To give does not always mean parting with material things, but more a desire to be concerned about others, to offer a hand to one in need, to be kind, understanding and forgiving when others do not do what we want or expect of them. There are many hidden forms of selfishness we need to detect and destroy in our journey from sense to Soul.

Being opinionated: One who is opinionated is opposed to accepting another view. He simply *knows* he is right. Usually the opinionated mentality is shaped not so much from facts, as from assumptions.

There is the claim of being so strongly opinionated that no change can take place in one's thinking. Such an opinionated mind will go to all lengths to prove it is right. One may even take pride in being obstinate and difficult, and will go into diatribes against issues or persons against which he holds a strong negative opinion. How can the qualities of the Second Degree unfold in a mental atmosphere so hardened in stubborn, antagonistic personal views?

But when we stop justifying our human opinions and learn to accept the fact that other views can be correct, or at least worth considering, we begin to be flexible, slow to judge, willing to wait on God to unfold the right view of things.

It is a great relief when we learn that we do not have to form an opinion about everything or everyone we come in contact with. Persons, events, things, can drift in and out of thought without our deciding — we like it or don't like it; he's right or he's wrong; it is good or it is bad. We learn to remain uncommitted to a view until we know the facts.

Self-righteousness: The self-righteous individual is convinced he is *always right*. He may even take a martyred attitude that his role in life is "to straighten everyone out." He can never admit to being wrong or making a mistake. He can be narrow-minded in what he considers to be right, intolerant of any differing views, and even belligerent with those who hold them.

When a person has this false trait, his mind is impervious to divine ideas, for the purpose of spiritual unfoldment is to correct wrong thinking, and one who is "always right" cannot even admit that such correction is needed.

As we progress in Christian Science, our views are constantly changing. What seems so right at one time becomes obsolete as we "put off the old man." But if we can never admit we can be wrong, the mind is closed to change of any kind. It will not let go of the old, and let the new unfold. Because mental blindness is antagonistic to progressive views, the self-righteous mind can be very argumentative, fighting change, contradicting and correcting others, putting them down. This leads to bickering, arguing, fighting, and as long as animal magnetism can keep us fighting with each other, it remains in control.

Stubbornness: The stubborn disposition is the essence of self-will. It is obstinate, unreasonable, perversely unyielding. The stubborn individual may take pride in being stubborn. He holds to his way of doing things and his views of life with the total conviction that he is always right, and it is impossible to try to reason with him. How can God reach a mind which refuses to change?

Being judgmental: It is not spiritually scientific to sit in judgment of another, to make comparisons, to criticize and condemn another through personal opinion. Too often we make wrong, even harsh, judgments based on incomplete facts and false assumptions. Mrs. Eddy once said, "God is giving each of us the experience best adapted to lead us to Him." Someone we presume to judge may be going through a difficult spiritual lesson, and we only add to his struggle by judging and condemning him. We are often most loving when we mind our own business and leave others alone. The habit of judging others is a violation of the law of Love.

28

Egotism: The egotistical mentality is filled with conceit, an exaggerated sense of self-importance and arrogance. This is a mental state that is impervious to spiritual unfoldment until some suffering experience humbles it. Egotism obstructs spiritual progress. Sometimes a student of Christian Science will gain the letter and perhaps some working knowledge of Science, and this causes him to be handled by egotism. His understanding stagnates at this point, for he does not have the humility that will bring him further unfoldment. Sooner or later the egotist encounters problems he cannot solve through his present understanding of Science, and he is forced to learn humility.

Pride: Pride is a form of self-centeredness. It is excessive self-esteem, conceit, haughtiness. It can be supercilious and condescending to others. The proud mentality assumes the right to look down on others as beneath him, to talk to them and treat them as inferior. Pride is often cold and cruel. It is found in all walks of life. Sometimes those who have the least, are insufferably proud and arrogant.

Pride and egotism are a great obstacle to spiritual progress. As students of Christian Science are successful to some degree in healing themselves and others, they sometimes allow a subtle form of pride and egotism to handle them and this stifles any further progress in Science.

Irritation: Being irritated, annoyed, peeved, ill-tempered with others — even though we may feel quite justified in being so — such common human faults cause chronic physical problems that can be very painful. An irritated state of mind is a form of low-key, habitual hatred and hostility. This subtle form of hatred may never be expressed in   outbursts of anger or open fighting, but the constant presence of irritation, disapproval, negativity, felt either secretly or openly by others, is habitual malpractice and violates the law of Love.

Impatience: This false trait usually comes from thwarted self-will that is intolerant of delay, opposition, or obstacles to what it wants or expects of others. Impatience can go from irritation to anger to rage over having to wait for any reason. It puts pressure on others by being aggressive, restless, agitated, ill-tempered with them. An impatient mentality is often impetuous or impulsive. This trait is seldom classified as sin, and yet it is a deadly sin. Habitual impatience can lead to difficult, stubborn, even seemingly incurable, physical problems.

Hatred: We can define hatred as intense hostility that usually comes from fear, anger, or a sense of mental, emotional or physical injury. We should search the inner self carefully for any hostility we may be holding towards even one person or one thing, for hatred comes in many guises.

It is important to consider the subtle, lesser forms of hatred that, undetected, harden the inner self. Are there moments of anger, hostility and unforgiveness in little things — a neighbor's children who litter our yard, a motorist who cuts us off, a friend's unkind remarks about us to another? When we react to such things with anger and hatred, we believe that some good has been taken from us — even if it is only our momentary peace of mind. Flashes of anger, habitual unforgiveness, continual dislike of certain people or things, hostility that takes control of our emotions — these continually darken the heart and mind.

Sometimes we simply have a habit of hating. We may not hate any person, but we hate our world, the weather, having to buy groceries, and get gas for the car. We hate certain responsibilities, obligations, legitimate demands made upon us. How often do we have a negative feeling towards the present moment? the place we are in? the people around us? Do we have an on-going hostility towards the circumstances and people that make up our daily experience? This negative attitude towards the entire fabric of our life, is a violation of the law of Love.

30

Especially difficult to overcome is *justified hatred*, which is the result of things said or done to us that are unjust and undeserved, and there is no regret or apology on the part of the offender. We do not imagine these wrongs, and so we feel justified in harboring hatred, unforgiveness, bitterness, and resentment. We seem unable to forgive and forget. And perhaps we are humanly justified in this. But so long as we allow such feelings to harden our mind, we will remain in mental darkness, filled with accumulating resentment, hurt feelings, grief, anger, disappointment, and even revenge.

When we learn that all that is good comes directly from God to us, we rise above hating. As we progress spiritually, as we learn to stop hating, to forgive and forget wrongs done to us, we overcome a main obstacle to demonstrating the Second Degree, and we eventually find that we are incapable of hatred.

Malice: Malice is the desire to see another suffer, a wish to see him in pain, injured, or in distress. We may be inclined to bypass this false trait, but if so, we need to ask ourselves: How often do we feel a secret sense of satisfaction when someone who competes with us suffers a set-back or misfortune — even a small one? How often do we feel superior or pleased when someone we do not like is defeated or we defeat them? especially if it vindicates our point of view or position? Do we enjoy reading about and watching drama which portrays suffering, pain, mental or physical cruelty? Are we fascinated by the malicious acts of another? Our identification with any form of malice first or second hand would suggest that latent within are unrecognized traces of this antichrist emotion.

Domination: The dominating will is determined to rule or control others. It demands obedience, and is intolerant of another's rights or views. This extreme form of self-will assumes the right to run other people's lives. It will not endure being crossed, and will punish anyone who does so. Aggressive, indomitable, insistent, it

31

forces others to comply to its demands, and denounces and shuts out those who will not allow themselves to be dominated.

A dominating personality usually considers itself a *very good* person. It is convinced that its motives are for the good of everyone and they are right in directing, manipulating, or forcing others to "do what is right" or "what is best for them." This hardened, insensitive state of mind usually experiences a great deal of suffering before it yields to the law of Love.

Anger: Wrath, rage, indignation — all forms of anger — are a manifestation of inflamed hatred due to thwarted self-will. We may not be perpetually angry about things, but how often do we flare up over something another does that "makes us mad"? Both hot, aggressive anger, and cold, silent anger, are forms of animal magnetism that completely silence the voice of God.

Criticism: The universal habit of saying unkind, unjust things about others is a prime violation of the law of Love. Criticism is a subtle form of hatred, yet it is so common that we seldom pause to consider how unchristian it is. Criticism is a relentless pastime of so many. They incessantly criticize everything and everyone.

It is a form of hatred to stress the faults of another, to ridicule or scorn him. To discuss, judge, dislike, or condemn another is to dwell on a false image of man. Constantly rehearsing personal offenses, harboring hostility and indignation, making personal attacks on another over assumed slights or misunderstandings, or resenting a lack of respect and thoughtfulness we feel is due us, is to shut out the Christ-consciousness. Often this is considered *justified* criticism because of the wrong we have endured from another; but all criticism is a violation of the law of Love.

Special care should be given to guarding against the silent, hidden thoughts and emotions that can occupy our thoughts *even though they go unsaid*. We must leave criticism *un-thought* and *un-felt*. Only when we stop malpracticing on others can we begin to understand and live the law of Love.

Ingratitude: If we assume that the generosity of another is something owed us, and we have little or no gratitude to him for giving to us, we remain selfish and insensitive to the effort made by another to help us. When we are ungrateful to others for their thoughtfulness, then we do not acknowledge God's goodness either. His infinite blessings will not unfold if we do not acknowledge the good already received. The stolid, ungrateful heart does not acknowledge God's gracious blessings because it is blind to them.

Unforgiveness: This trait is a passive form of hatred. Perhaps we cannot or do not choose to retaliate for unjust or cruel treatment, yet we feel we cannot forgive another for what he has done to us. We punish others and make them feel guilty when we do not forgive them, for they feel the criticism, hostility, hate and resentment we hold towards them.

We may believe we cannot stop resenting the wrongs done us. A certain amount of unforgiveness seems a normal part of life. Yet rehearsing these wrongs and resenting them is to make a reality of them, and this accumulated resentment, hurt, anger — all the negative emotions that come with unforgiveness — will obstruct our entrance into the kingdom of God.

Revenge: We think of revenge as an obvious act of hate, vindicating a wrong that deserves to be punished. But a secret desire for revenge can lodge within when we feel another has wronged us. Most of us would not plan to deliberately inflict mental, emotional, or physical pain on another in retaliation for something done to us. But we can "punish" him by being unpleasant, uncooperative, difficult, aloof. We may manage somehow to make things hard for him. We may take secret satisfaction in a defeat or misfortune he experiences, even though it was not our doing. Even wanting revenge or wishing some misfortune for him is to harbor hatred and unforgiveness towards another.

Jealousy, envy, emulation: Human ambition to be successful, and the competition and rivalry that it usually takes to do so, can bring about jealousy. We become possessive of our position, belongings, friends, and family. This generates a suspicious, hostile attitude towards anyone who threatens our success and its rewards. False ambition causes envy — the coveting of those things that belong to another. It brings on emulation — ambitious or envious rivalry. This intensely competitive mental state is the result of materialism and false ambition. We rise above rivalry and false ambition as we learn that good is infinite, and that God unfolds unlimited good to everyone. If everyone has infinite good, this rules out all cause for jealousy, envy, and emulation.

Disappointment: We are disappointed when we look to persons and not to God for every good thing. Disappointment comes through personal sense. When others do not live up to their promises or do not do what we expect of them, when we plan and outline certain things and they do not come to pass, we feel hurt, resentful, rejected, depressed. We may not be rewarded or appreciated for work well done. Others may not acknowledge or reciprocate our gifts, our generosity, our unselfish help. There are many causes for disappointment; and fed by the constant rehearsal of unjust experiences or circumstances, it can a become a state of chronic sadness and rejection. But as we learn to look to God for every good thing, we find disappointment and depression lessening until it disappears.

Self-justification: When we disobey the law of Love, we feel we must justify it to ourselves and others. We excuse or explain or plead our right to be unkind, revengeful, disrespectful to another. We argue that we were entitled to do what we did because of what was done to us. When we must convince ourselves or others that an unkind word or act on our part was right, we have violated the law of Love. This habit of justifying and excusing wrong-doing blinds us to the difference between right and wrong and keeps us in the First Degree.

Rebelliousness: To be rebellious is to defy authority, to oppose and resist any kind of control. Some individuals cannot conform to the rules of society. Quite often, when a rebellious person is forced to conform, he resorts to punishing the authority by being difficult, sullen and uncooperative.

While we may conform to the rules of society, we should carefully consider whether we rebel at the more demanding requirements of the Second Degree. If we lack self-discipline and a willingness to obey God, if we defy the moral and spiritual laws, we justify this by believing that it is too difficult to live such "regimented" lives.

Dishonesty: A careful monitoring of our daily words and deeds, may reveal many unconscious commitments of dishonesty that are accepted as part of getting through the day.

We think of dishonesty as the intent to cheat or rob another, or to deliberately lie or commit fraud. But there are many shades of dishonesty that an individual may practice without realizing it. At times he may pervert or suppress the truth or misrepresent facts. Exaggeration, hypocrisy, flattery, deception, are dishonest. Manipulating others or leading them to believe things that are not entirely true, making promises that we do not fully intend to keep, using another's trust or innocence or ignorance to our advantage, being secretive about information another should know — all of these are practiced daily by many who consider themselves honest. Every half-truth, every little lie, used to get us what we want or to avoid a confrontation, are examples of dishonesty. And Mrs. Eddy says, "Dishonesty . . . forfeits God's help."

Fear: Fear is so universal it is seldom, if ever, classified as sin; yet it comes from the solid conviction in a power apart from God. Fear permeates modern day living, causing anxiety, insecurity, worry, stress, care, nervousness, despair, dismay, dread, sickness, disease, death. Because we do not understand that God is all and evil is unreal, we are handled by every kind of fear — fear of sickness, disease, age, accidents, catastrophes, adversity, things going wrong; fear of criticism, disapproval, being unloved and alone, misunderstood; fear of lack and failure; fear of material laws; fear of the future, foods, weather, germs and virus; fear for our family, our church, our country. The fears of today seem beyond numbering.

Some individuals live behind a wall of fear their entire lifetime. Fear is due to ignorance of God and His power to care for us. To the fearful mind, the entire universe seems hostile and negative, and he sees himself a victim of material laws and conditions, imprisoned in a life of danger and limitation, constantly threatened by a dark, ominous, ungodlike mental force over which he seems to have no control.

The anxiety, nervousness and insecurity produced by fear are manifested in sickness and disease. We should give much time to recognizing and handling the many claims of fear that we have been conditioned to accept as natural and necessary for our good. Eventually we must demonstrate over all fear. We can begin now by handling each fear as we recognize it. With each victory over some specific fear, we are a little closer to being free of all fear.

Being dominated: Often one who is controlled and manipulated by the domination of another appears to be a helpless victim forced to submit to another's indomitable will. Actually, one is a victim of another's control because of his *fear*. A dominating person seeks someone to dominate, and a fearful, insecure person allows another to dominate him. The dominated individual will keep the peace by giving in to the other — often believing he is being loving by doing so. But being controlled by the self-will of another is just as wrong as acting through our own self-will. It is not normal to be intimidated and controlled by another. The dominated person needs to handle fear in himself — not the self-will of another.

When someone is dominated, he must suppress his own individuality to keep from being the target of the hatred and anger of the one dominating him. This thwarted state of mind produces many severe physical and emotional and mental problems. The dominated individual cannot find his freedom until he overcomes his fear and learns to be independently dependent on God alone for all things.

Self-pity: We are filled with self-pity when we believe that we are shut out of infinite good. Others have love, companionship, family, affluence, success, while we have been denied these things. We count ourselves among the "have-nots." We believe that we are deprived of the freedom to do what we want to do, and the means to have what we should have.

When those to whom we show love and generosity never acknowledge our giving, and there is no reciprocation, or when we do our best and it is misunderstood, criticized, belittled, we feel sorry for ourselves. The reasons for self-pity are many. But our disappointment and unhappiness are caused by looking to persons rather than God for all things. Instead of accepting the claim of being deprived and unappreciated, why not enlarge our understanding of God until we demonstrate over this mesmerism that holds us down in the First Degree? Is it not a sin to believe that the divine Principle, Love, is partial and would give more to one than another?

Guilt: Those handled by guilt, see only their own faults, failings, inadequacies — often greatly magnified. They may blame and condemn themselves for everything that goes wrong — even when they are not at fault. Such self-condemnation and self-hatred is a form of self-malpractice. They believe they are not good enough to be loved, accepted, or successful. Out of habit they may constantly feel guilty for no reason at all.

Guilt can be caused by prolonged association with a dominating person who constantly abuses and denounces one. The victim is made to feel he is the cause of another's problems. He becomes a scapegoat, and believes there is nothing right about himself, that he cannot do anything right, say anything right. And so he comes to condemn himself and even hate himself. He is made to feel guilty, to see only his own faults and failings. While he seems the victim of another's malpractice, it is really his own fear and submission to the abuse of another that blinds him to his oneness with God.

Inferiority complex: Inferiority may be expressed in great timidity — being shy, withdrawn, unable to relate easily to others. A sensitive individual takes everything personally, and believes he is being blamed for all that goes wrong. He is easily hurt, disappointed, depressed, dejected for the slightest reason. He is extremely self-conscious, and lives in unrelieved fear.

Another form of inferiority will over-compensate for a sense of inadequacy through exaggerated aggressiveness. He will not admit to having any faults or to ever being wrong, but is obsessed with the faults of others and their insensitive inconsideration of him. He will take great satisfaction and pleasure in seeing others fail, as such failure gives him a momentary sense of superiority. He may even cause or contribute to the failure of others in order to make them feel inferior.

Whatever form an inferiority complex takes, it needs to be corrected with a true understanding of man in God's likeness.

Persecution complex: This is a state of mind wherein the individual believes that others are plotting against him, threatening, harassing, persecuting him — even when there is no real evidence of it. He is certain that "they" are intentionally planning to injure him. He claims to be affected mentally, if not physically, by their presence; he knows "they" are trying to disturb, trouble, even torment him. He is often hostile towards others, angry, defensive, quick to accuse others and defend himself.

Too often the persecution is imaginary — especially if it follows him from place to place, or if others in the same situation or place do not feel harassed or threatened. This ingrained belief is very stubborn to overcome, for the individual is convinced he is being spied upon and persecuted, but no one will believe him.

A false sense of responsibility: This false trait is one of human goodness wherein a responsible person feels he must help others with their responsibilities and obligations, take on their burdens and problems, because they will not or cannot do so. He will worry excessively about other people's problems, interfere in their affairs in an effort to help them. He then feels burdened because he has both their problems and his own. There are those who take unfair advantage of such kindness. So long as one is willing to do for them, they will let him — often imposing, expecting, even demanding, that he help them in their on-going trials and tribulations. It is not God's plan that the hard working Scientist be overburdened with the responsibility for others because he has Science and they do not. Often in assuming others' responsibilities in the desire to be needed or useful, he deprives them of their own unfoldment and development.

Human goodness: As we progress in Christian Science, we learn that human goodness is not enough to save us from the suffering caused by animal magnetism, because the humanly good person still believes in the reality of evil.

There is a type of human goodness, sweetness and affection coupled with innocence, dearness and goodness, that seems almost saintly. It requires protection from the world. But too often a protected individual is so disturbed and pained by the seeming reality of animal magnetism — the suffering and agony of man's inhumanity to man — that he cannot bear to face it. This is not a spiritual state of mind. It is an extreme form of fear and mortal sensitivity. Such a mentality wants to look away from evil and error, rather than face it, see through it and demonstrate dominion over it. He may believe that he cannot handle it.

If through human sentiment, goodness, innocence and sweetness, one avoids any unpleasant struggle with error, then he avoids all hard experiences. He seems to lack the strength and wisdom that come from coping daily with error and demonstrating over it. Thus when a difficult claim seems to manifest itself, he goes through a very suffering experience.

The purpose of Christian Science is to enable one to face even the most aggressive forms of evil with spiritual strength and understanding, and reduce them to nonexistence. The spiritual love demonstrated in the Second Degree is *strong* and *courageous* as well as pure.

Making a great reality of the world's evil and suffering: The humanly good person would not do anything wrong himself, but sometimes he is obsessed with the state of the world — a doom and gloom picture of the future of humanity in which there is no hope for the triumph of good over evil. He makes a great reality of other's sins. He is honest himself, but distressed over the dishonesty, crime, discord, drugs, divorce, disease and the suffering of others. In making such a reality of evil, he cannot discern the activity of Truth that is also taking place.

Intellectualism: An intellectual mind may assume that an intellectual pursuit of Christian Science will enable him to understand it in the way he has come to understand academic subjects. He may confuse an intellectual mastering of the letter of Science with spirituality. But the exercise of intellect without the inspiration of love does not unfold the advanced understanding of Science. It will not substitute for the study of Science permeated with the spiritual love of the Second Degree.

The study of Christian Science is intended to develop divine intelligence. When the desire to understand God is permeated with spiritual love, the mind is open to the unfoldment of spiritual ideas. Then as we study and pray, our intelligence is transformed through the unfoldment of ideas that God gives us. We measure our spiritual intelligence by our ability to heal. It requires both intelligence and love to understand Christian Science.

Sensualism: When we are obsessed with bodily enjoyment, sensuous pleasures, creature comforts that amount to ease in matter, we are living for gratification of the senses. Passion and appetites, sensuous and emotional experiences, are magnetic in drawing us away from God. It is not the pain of the senses, but the pleasures of the senses that hold us in the First Degree.

Complaining: The habit of complaining, whining, fretting and grumbling — is any mortal trait more universal than the continuous moan, "Nothing is right"? When we are fretful, complaining constantly over things that annoy and irritate us, we make such a reality of them that the mind is always in a negative, disturbed, restless, agitated, discontented state.

When we complain and fret, we are denying the allness of God. What good is it to study and pray for a certain amount of time each day, claiming the allness of God and the unreality of evil, only to close the books and join the chorus of the complaining multitudes? Endless complaining insists that evil is real and misfortune the lot of man. We can hardly be receptive to God's thoughts while we are constantly denying His presence and power, and making such a reality of animal magnetism.

Materialism: Many of us would not consider ourselves materialistic or worldly in the narrow sense of the word. But how often are we more interested in the material world than in the world of Spirit? Do we mistake a prosperous and comfortable mortal life for the demonstration of spiritual understanding?

Attraction to the evils of animal magnetism: The gravitational pull of animal magnetism attracts the human mind towards the gross, vulgar, loud, profane, sensual, and materialistic world of the senses. The human mind is fascinated by the audacity of evil. A desire to know what evil is doing results in mental pollution. A polluted mind is filled with the images of evil's seeming aggressiveness, power, success, and reality.

Although we may not be personally involved in the materialism and grossness of animal magnetism, we may be intrigued with watching it. We may amuse ourselves by seeing, reading, and hearing about the sins of others. We are entertained by the fiction that dramatizes the mental and physical cruelty, abuse, brutality, horror, sexuality and grossness of animal magnetism. Evil is so vividly portrayed in the media that it seems to be more real and powerful than Truth.

Being mesmerized by the power and pleasure of materialism and sensualism hardens the mind until it becomes rocklike. The inner self is so darkened by the constant absorption of error that it is impervious to the influence of God's thoughts. It must first turn from this interest in animal magnetism, shut it out, and strive to reflect divine Love in order to escape from the First Degree.

Irresponsibility: The irresponsible person is changeable, fickle, weak, unreliable, lacking in self-discipline. He can be uncooperative, lazy, apathetic, even perverse and demanding. Lacking a sense of responsibility, he will say and do things with no concern for the consequences to himself or others. Unable to conform to even the ordinary demands of society, he must learn self-discipline before he can conform to the law of Love.

False ambition: This mortal trait is driven to succeed in the material world. It is a preoccupation with material wealth, power, importance, and recognition.

Miserliness: The claim of a frugal, miserly, overly thrifty mind is either extremely selfish or is consumed with the fear of lack, or both. Until this fear is healed, this tight, close, limited mentality cannot express the generosity, openness, joy and freedom of the Second Degree.

Quarreling: Conflict, bickering, haggling, contradicting, and disagreeing with others and putting them down out of habit — this needs to be carefully considered. If we quarrel with others, we will quarrel with God.

Sarcasm, ridiculing, needling, teasing, belittling and putting down others, purposely misleading and confusing them; being contentious, disagreeable, difficult, in order to control others or make them react; a negative attitude towards life in general: These are all common sins that are forms of hatred and are void of spiritual love.

Refusing to admit one has any of these faults: This is in itself a universal form of animal magnetism that we must handle. A false sense of human goodness can be extremely difficult to overcome.

Refusing to look within because one does not want to face the many faults he knows he has.

The traits or sins in this list have been defined in their most obvious and aggressive forms, but they can be present in very subtle, devious, hidden ways that we do not recognize when we first start the work of inner transformation. Even the best human nature has elements of self-will, hatred and fear that are universally accepted as normal. But as we progress in Science, the most hidden sins come to light to be destroyed.

43

This list is long and thought-provoking. It may seem to some readers shocking and overwhelming, for few of us have ever considered these traits as sinful. But seen as a violation of the law of Love, we begin to understand and demonstrate Christian Science more effectively. The presence of sin in consciousness hardens thought to the spiritual unfoldment that God waits to give us. Unless we recognize these common sins, they continue to harden the mind, deaden spiritual intuition, and paralyze the flow of divine ideas.

If we avoid acknowledging that we have any of these mortal traits, we need to realize that it is the nature of personal sense to fight against its own destruction. Animal magnetism's strongest hold on us is through false traits that seem normal, even desirable, and especially through those hardest to detect and overcome.

The Penalties for Sin

Our personality is made up of thought-habits that image themselves forth in a pattern of mortal life that remains basically the same throughout a lifetime. Our human mentality is the only one we have ever known. We live in it as a our normal state of mind, and the false thought-habits imprison us in the same familiar problems year after year. An angry mind will seek out things to be angry about. A dominating mind will relate to others through dominating them. A fretful mind will find endless little things to fret over. An irritated mind will imagine sources of irritation everywhere. A fearful mind will feel threatened by many things that never bother others.

The constant discord and unhappiness that chronic sin generates, is unfortunate in itself. But disobedience to God also produces sickness, disease, lack, limitation, discordant relationships, age, adversity, accidents, and ultimately death.

Mankind has not attached severe penalties to common sins. There are legal penalties for breaking the laws of the land. In recent years certain health penalties have been recognized in the use of drugs, alcohol, caffeine, and tobacco.

But no penalty has been recognized for the common sins of hatred, self-will, domination, fear — all of the emotions that violate the law of Love. It would seem that there are no penalties resulting from habitual animosity towards others, criticism and disapproval, fear and anxiety, or self-will, self-righteousness and self-justification. Yet God's laws are penal laws. They carry with them some form of punishment when they are broken. The punishment of sin is inevitable, for Mrs. Eddy writes in *Science and Health*, "Without punishment, sin would multiply." The punishment of such disobedience to God is the seemingly incurable problems that will not yield to our metaphysical work. Sinful traits produce mental and emotional illness, incurable diseases and functional disorders, lack, limitation, senility and death.

I have known individuals with an indomitable will and temper. They go through life forcing others to do what they want. In time they have paid the penalty for a lifetime of such sin. Some have slowly lost their memory. They cannot remember something told them a minute before. They literally lose their minds. Others with dominating natures have been so crippled by arthritis that they cannot even feed themselves. Others have paralyzing strokes.

I have seen those who have accumulated a strong justified hatred for others whom they feel have wronged them. These unforgiving, bitter, angry emotions have resulted in cancer and other diseases that are painful and fatal.

I have seen those so fearful and so dominated that they completely suppress their natural selfhood in order to placate others and keep the peace. This has often resulted in asthma, skin conditions, heart disease, and a number of other seemingly incurable disorders.

Age, decrepitude and senility are not the work of time. They are due to forms of sin that have gradually become manifested in the disease of old age. The physical and mental suffering that precedes death is the penalty for breaking spiritual laws. What punishment there may be after death, we know not.

It is not scientific to say certain traits cause certain diseases and disorders. It is essential, however, to look through and beyond the physical problem to the sin causing it. Diseases, disorders, mental and emotional pain, are the penalties we pay for disobedience to God.

Billions of dollars are spent annually on medical research into the cause and cure of diseases. But disease in one form or another continues, and is even increasing, because the hidden cause — the sins that defy God's laws — have become more aggressive in recent decades. Disease is on the increase and will only decline and disappear as sin is forsaken.

Until we see sin as the cause of disease, disease will continue to take on new and more mysterious forms, and will seem incurable. Unless we see the cause as sinful traits, we will wonder why we cannot meet certain chronic problems in Christian Science.

When we seem to have a physical problem that will not heal, it is useless to handle it as a disease or illness, for the problem is the *effect* of sin. So long as hatred, fear, selfishness or other causes go unchallenged, the effects will either remain, or leave only to return, often in a more severe form. The fear *is* the disease. The hatred *is* the disease.

When we recognize and overcome a false trait, we heal the discordant effects it produces; we also *prevent* the harmful effects of sin, before they become a physical claim.

This point is not explored enough in Christian Science. Too often when we are sick, we handle a *physical* problem. If we fail to heal, it is because we are handling disease instead of *sin.* We mistake when we handle cancer, heart trouble, eyesight, hearing, age, etc. These are the *effects of sin.* Often they are the results of a sin of long standing that has gone undetected and uncorrected until at last it becomes manifested on the body as disease.

46

No disease or physical problem arbitrarily forms itself in matter and attacks us, manifesting itself on the body for no apparent reason. It originates in the inner self, and is imaged forth from a mortal mentality.

Throughout her writings, Mrs. Eddy refers to "sin, disease, death" in that order. The word *sin* is used to define disobedience to God. Sin defies God's laws. Prolonged sin results in disease, and death comes because of it. In order to prevent disease and overcome death, it is necessary to define the endless subtle forms of sin that seem to control us almost involuntarily. We ignorantly sin in many ways because we do not realize the full meaning of the word.

We may believe that all sin is obvious, so obvious that we cannot miss detecting it. On the contrary, the subtle forms of sin that cause the good person to suffer are more than we can imagine. I have often been astonished at the extremely painful claims of disease and physical malfunctions that come from small, seemingly insignificant, or justified forms of ungodlike thoughts and emotions that claim to be a part of what we call normal consciousness.

I have seen many instances where a person who considers himself to be an exemplary Christian Scientist, comes under a stubborn claim. He will work diligently to meet it as a physical problem, but with no success. He is completely baffled, because he has not learned to treat sin, rather than disease. As a rule, he has been ignorantly violating the law of Love for a long period of time — perhaps a lifetime. This mental disobedience may have been through ignorance; but even so, it has eventually brought about a form of disease that will not heal until the sin has been recognized, and he has reformed his thinking.

Because the sinful thinking has been going on for many years and the disease is perhaps recent, the person does not see the connection between the two. If he cannot or will not recognize the sinful trait causing the problem and correct it, the disease will not yield to his mental work.

47

We see, therefore, that detecting and casting off mortal elements of sin brings about a double blessing. The inner self becomes receptive to the spiritual ideas that lead us into the kingdom within, and the mind is healed of sinful habits that cause disease, lack, discord, adversity, and death.

The Basic Cause of Sin and Disease

Just as disease is the effect of sinful mortal traits, so mortal traits are in themselves the *effect* of the belief in the reality and power of evil and matter. From belief in evil comes the ignorance, fear, hate and selfishness that shut us out of the spiritual realm. Christian Science healing is based on the fact that evil, sin, disease, and death are illusions of mortal mind. They are not real. However we may *say* there is no evil or matter, but *there still remains in the heart of consciousness the concrete conviction that evil and matter are so powerful that they hold the issues of life and death for us.*

We cannot begin too soon to learn to handle animal magnetism as the cause of false traits. The purpose of our work in Christian Science, is to understand the allness of God and the nothingness of evil. *As we wrestle with the conviction that evil is real, we de-mesmerize consciousness of this false conviction and the traits that are rooted in it.*

It would be a relief to by-pass this struggle with evil, but we do not have that choice. We may avoid this fight because we fear the ordeal of facing evil and facing it down. But the result of this work gives us a dominion that is awesome. Once we gather the courage to resist evil, and we continue to do so, we discover that *it really is nothing.* We also find that as the conviction in evil's reality diminishes, the sinful traits also begin to fall away, and the suffering that they produce vanishes like a dream. Therefore,

48

by wrestling with the conviction that evil is real, we begin to transform our present state of mind and emerge out of the First Degree.

Reformation Possible in Christian Science

We cannot reform the heart and mind without the Science which enables us to do so. It is useless to tell one to stop being afraid, to stop hating, to stop being selfish and difficult. He must be convinced of the need to do so, and he must be given a way to reform the inner self. With Christian Science, he can actually transcend a mortal personality. Through study and prayer, he can handle not only the false emotions, but the fundamental cause — the belief in the reality and power of evil and matter.

Christian Science is an advanced intelligence that gives the mind something to change to. The mind cannot progress unless there is a more enlightened state of thought to replace the old.

Our work in Science takes on new depth and meaning when we begin to treat specific forms of sin. We no longer have to wait until these false traits cause us to suffer, and we are forced to demonstrate over them. We can take the initiative and grapple with them *now*. And in doing so, we prevent the need to suffer out of them.

If we accept the fact that we must change our thought-habits, can we do so? Yes, there is no mind so hardened that it cannot change. There are no mortal emotions impervious to divine Love. As Christian Science is introduced into consciousness, a new, more advanced concept of God and man begins to purify thought. The more we understand and live Science, the purer our thought. This Science first separates the mortal from the immortal. It clearly defines the nature of each, and then provides the form of prayer that can actually change or transform consciousness.

The initial change comes when we make a deep and total commitment to understand Christian Science. This alone begins to soften consciousness.

As we study and pray, we enter the spiritual realm by degrees. Gradually our love becomes pure, strong, and constant, our thought softens, and the advanced spiritual understanding appears as our own revelation of Truth. The results of this work are different from what we might expect. We become extremely happy, joyous, peaceful, active, creative, warm, safe, loving, affluent, free. We do not yield up our mortal selfhood for a lonely, stringent, 'saintly' life. We find the kingdom within to be what it is promised to be — heavenly.

Chapter IV

THE SECOND DEGREE
SPIRITUAL LOVE

We have known and believed the love that
God hath to us. God is Love; he that dwelleth
in love dwelleth in God, and God in him.

JOHN

The way to extract error from mortal mind is
to pour in Truth through flood-tides of Love.
Christian perfection is won on no other
basis.

MARY BAKER EDDY

The mortal personality does not naturally reform itself. It is a well-known fact that analyzing negative emotions and beliefs will not change them to any extent, even when we know they are sickness-producing. That is why detecting animal magnetism in ourselves and others does not destroy it. It is not an analysis of error, but an understanding of God, that heals and regenerates. We do need to see the errors to be overcome; but to transform consciousness, we need a good reason to change, and a higher form of intelligence to change to. Only then do we begin to transcend our present state of mind.

Christian Science specifically defines the nature of mortal mind and animal magnetism and shows both to be unreal. It also accurately defines God, and the spiritual nature of man and the universe. Since good and evil are opposite states of mind, the belief in evil is eliminated from consciousness as we understand the nature of God, for we cannot have both in the same mind at the same time. Through study and prayer, we begin to exchange the false traits of the First Degree for the moral qualities of the Second, which is defined as "Evil Beliefs Disappearing."

Second Degree Analyzed

Let us carefully consider the terms used in defining the Second Degree: humanity, honesty, affection, compassion, hope, faith, meekness, temperance. Again as we read these terms, we may *assume* that we already express them enough to be well-established in the Transitional Stage. Undoubtedly we already do express most of these qualities to some extent. But a limited or meager practice of them is not acceptable if we are to become healing metaphysicians. Is your present thought so softened by these qualities that you consider yourself capable of meeting every challenge you face through spiritual means alone? Doing the work yourself without help from another? We measure our spirituality by our healing works, and a mind filled with the qualities of the Second Degree and enlightened with the letter of Christian Science is able to overcome extremely challenging claims through its own prayerful work. Surely we do express the Christly qualities of affection, honesty, hope, faith, but do we have them in the depth and strength necessary to soften the heart and mind and make it receptive to the more profound ideas that God waits to give us?

Let us analyze these qualities to determine how essential they are in freeing us from the First Degree.

Humanity: We do not as a rule associate this term with our personal lives. It has been used more to designate those who give of their time and money to help others less fortunate. A humanitarian is one who promotes human welfare and social reform. And yet Mrs. Eddy begins the Second Degree with this word *humanity*.

Humanity means being humane, kind, caring. It stands for

affectionate feelings, compassion, sympathy and consideration for others. It includes the desire to relieve stress and suffering and to treat all life with loving compassion and consideration — and that includes your wife or husband, your children and parents, your relatives and friends, everyone with whom you live, work, socialize or do business. If you do not express kindness and care towards those closest to you, it means that you do not really understand and practice humanity.

Have you ever considered how inhumane unspoken hatred and disapproval are? When we indulge in chronic irritation, annoyance, impatience, anger, or criticism towards others, it is a form of mental cruelty, affecting all within the atmosphere of our thought. Habitual one-upmanship, antagonism, domination, bickering, sarcasm, are expressions of inhumanity, and contrary to the law of Love. The desire to relieve stress and suffering applies to all our immediate relationships and situations. Are we sensitive to the feelings and needs of others? forgiving and understanding of the little things they do that could be annoying? Do we support them in their times of need — emotionally as well as physically and financially?

We must first be humane and caring consistently towards those close to us before we can be humane to the world at large. Our expression of love must be genuine. We cannot be civilized to those outside the home, and then be hateful, indifferent, demanding, and selfish at home behind closed doors. We must live humanity for everyone, everywhere, all the time. When we understand that all our good comes directly from God to us, and is not sifted through others, we can be kind, generous, forgiving, for we know we are secure in God's care. The demands and needs of others cannot deplete our good. Indeed, the more we give, the more freely God gives to us. Therefore, humanity is a quality that is basic to obeying the law of Love. We should measure all we think and say and do with the question, "Is it loving? kind? caring?"

Feb 10 2020

53

Honesty: What an interesting word for Mrs. Eddy to include in the Second Degree. Honesty destroys the duplicity of a mind that indulges in small deceits, innocent little lies, clever and undetected acts of manipulation. It is against the law of Love to deceive, exaggerate, flatter, and use others. This word means much more than honorably meeting our obligations — financial and otherwise. It applies to *all* of our dealings with others — including those nearest and dearest to us. Honesty means being fair and straightforward with others. It includes justice, sincerity, integrity, trustworthiness, accuracy and reliability.

We need to think carefully about this word *honesty*. We may want to gloss over it, assuming we understand what it means, but it is rather shocking, when we begin to analyze honesty, to realize how much we have to learn about it.

We hear today about honesty being relevant, suggesting that there are gray areas where half-truths and subtle forms of deceit are acceptable, even necessary, to get along in the world. But Mrs. Eddy shows that there can be no compromise with our practice of honesty. In her article on obedience in *Miscellaneous Writings*, she writes, "Honesty in every condition, under every circumstance, is the indispensable rule of obedience." And in her *Message to The Mother Church for 1896*, she says, "Christian Scientists have a strong race to run, and foes in ambush; but bear in mind that, in the long race, honesty always defeats dishonesty." In *Science and Health* we read, "Dishonesty is human weakness, which forfeits divine help."

Complete honesty is essential to our spiritual unfoldment. As we explore the more refined ethics fundamental to the practice of Christian Science, we learn the difference between honesty and dishonesty in its most subtle forms. It sounds simple to be honest until we begin to measure *every* thought and word and deed against our highest concept of honesty. Are we given to half-truths, exaggerations? Do we ever try to influence others to do what we want, even if it is to their detriment? Do we pry into the personal affairs of others? Are we slightly unethical and deceitful in our business and personal lives? Do we do things that are dishonest if we know we will not be caught?

When we stop to analyze honesty in its purest form, we begin to see how often we ignorantly or unconsciously violate this transitional quality. Not only must our words and deeds be honest, our *thoughts* and *intentions* must be honest. Truth does not condone hypocrisy for any reason. We must be genuinely honest — void of duplicity.

Honesty, most of all, means being honest with yourself, admitting to yourself when certain thoughts and feelings — those most secretly hidden from others — are ungodlike, unloving. So often we *defend* and *justify* acts of deceit and dishonesty. We are handled by error when we do this. And while we do not have to confess such things to others, we do have to be honest enough in our inmost thoughts to acknowledge our violations of the law of Love to ourselves and correct them.

The ethics of Christian Science are plainly given in *Science and Health*. They include honesty, integrity, and respect for the rights of others; but the ethics of Christian Science go beyond the commonly accepted practice of these qualities. The Christian Scientist must respect and honor the right of each individual to govern his own mind free of the mental influence of another — whether silent or spoken. To influence or directly pray for another without his consent is dishonest. It can be a form of malpractice that is harmful to him; and it will eventually cost the one doing this mental work his ability to heal. We can correct our own thought about another's problem, but to intentionally treat another without his knowledge can be a mistaken sense of love and an abuse of Christian Science.

As you can see, honesty needs careful study; and we need to do much inner searching in relation to all aspects of honesty if we are to make a complete demonstration of this quality.

Affection: True affection transcends the personal and sensual love of the First Degree. It can be defined in such terms as gentleness, tenderness, kindness, generosity, thoughtfulness, understanding, patience and forgiveness. Unselfed love, sensitivity towards others, self-sacrificing for the good of others — these are the first indication of divine Love being imaged forth as our true nature.

Affection counteracts selfishness and self-love, and establishes our love on a higher plane — one that does not act or react with the emotionalism of mortal mind. It is our unselfish motives and acts that distinguish spiritual love from sensual, personal love. Affection is *always* kind, thoughtful, giving and forgiving.

When we think of love, it is usually to be *given* love, approval, kindness, loyalty, understanding, and support, to be admired, respected, cared for. We want to *find* love, *have* love, *be loved*. And while it is usually a personal love we seek, what we really yearn for is something more stable than human emotionalism.

 The fact is, we cannot feel the presence of spiritual love in others until we have cultivated some degree of it ourselves. One can be in the company of the purest and warmest love; but if he has little or no love within, he will not recognize that he is in the presence of such pure love.

If we are insensitive to spiritual love, we can not understand God as Love either. As long as we are in the Adam-dream, we see God and man in the image of our own mortal selfhood. If we are selfish and self-willed, we think of God as selfish and withholding, and see His will as forceful and unmerciful. If we are hateful, we see God as angry, cold, vindictive, punishing man for his sins. If we are fearful, we see God as tyrannical, sending unjust, undeserved difficulties and discord. We see both God and man in the image of our own mortal selfhood. Therefore, God may give abundantly of His ideas, but how can we recognize and accept them if we do not understand Him as divine Love? Can we know God's thoughts if we have not learned the meaning of affection?

Affection includes forgiveness. Forgiveness requires special thought, for it is essential to demonstrating the transitional stage. Forgiveness is one of the strongest expressions of true affection there is, and one of the hardest to learn. The unforgiving thought complains about the way it is treated; it is hurt, resentful, vindictive, upset over even the smallest slights. It is angry over what it considers mistakes, inefficiency or stupidity in others that affect it personally. It holds grudges. It is petty, mean and hateful. Prolonged unforgiveness becomes bitterness that turns the heart to stone.

When we forgive, we rise above self-pity, self-righteousness, resentment, anger, revenge — all that claims to be personal sense — and we forgive others for not loving us. We *forgive lovingly* and then *forget* the wrong. As we learn to be forgiving, we reach the point where we are seldom offended by what others say or do. If we are disturbed, we find we can get over any wrong committed against us quickly. To learn to be generous, forgiving, and affectionate towards everyone all the time unfolds the Christ-love within, softens the heart, and purifies the mental atmosphere we live in.

Compassion: This transitional quality has always been associated with the Christ-consciousness. It is closely akin to humanity and affection, in that it expresses kindness, caring, concern over another's suffering. We have compassion for anyone going through a severe problem; we are concerned, caring; we help if we can.

But if Mrs. Eddy included compassion in the Second Degree, it must be very important. It can mean the giving of yourself to those around you all the time. It is the activity of love in your relationships — supporting others, doing what you can to help them, getting involved if you have something that will meet another's need, being generous with what you have with those around you who need this help.

When we lack compassion, we are indifferent to others; we are stolid, passive; we stand by or walk on when we see some-

57

one in need of help. Even worse, we may add to another's suffering by judging or criticizing him in his trials. We may even berate him for getting into such difficulties.

We should express compassion towards those closest to us — our family and friends and associates. We can say or do the kind, caring thing when the opportunity comes, and leave *un*-said and *un*-done those things that add to their problems or create new ones for them.

Hope and Faith: These qualities are akin to each other. They are essential for entering the Third Degree. Recall that we are dependent on God for the spiritual ideas that transform consciousness. We cannot devise these ideas out of our own human intellect because they are different from what we now know. They appear in the mind softened by hope and faith and love.

When we have hope, we cherish the desire to know God, and we expect this desire to be fulfilled. The expectancy of spiritual inspiration and unfoldment *precedes* the appearing of spiritual ideas. Since we recognize Christian Science as the promised Comforter, what greater reason do we need for entertaining hope? This positive, receptive quality of hope softens the inner self, and brings about the unfoldment of spiritual ideas.

Faith also precedes the appearance of God's thoughts within. Faith is the acknowledgment that we do not yet understand divine reality, but we are capable of doing so and — even more important — that the answers that we are seeking actually exist in divine Mind. Although we do not yet entertain John's vision of a new heaven and earth, we can and eventually will, because it is our destiny to do so.

Faith recognizes spiritual realities and moral principles to be of paramount importance and supreme value. Humanity, affection, compassion show our love for man. Faith and hope show our love for God. They signify the light of spiritual understanding dawning in consciousness.

Meekness: Meekness is humility, and of this quality, Mrs. Eddy writes, "Humility is the genius of Christian Science." Again considering that we are dependent on God's thoughts in order to enter the kingdom within, we must echo Jesus' words, "Of mine own self I can do nothing." In the heart of prayer, we need to reason with ourselves as to how little we really understand and demonstrate of Christian Science — especially in the light of Christ Jesus' healings and Mrs. Eddy's many impressive demonstrations. Then in the depths of meekness, we can ask the Father to teach us what they knew that they could do such works. What was the understanding of God that illumined their minds and made their healing work so effortless?

Such humble prayer is almost unknown in today's world. Who today is meek? Everyone is storming about demanding their rights. Meekness is a rare quality, little understood and practiced by the world. It shows an absence of false pride, arrogance, personal opinion, pretense. It is the unselfed ego, the individuality void of personal sense.

Meekness also includes that wonderful quality — *patience*. Patience — like meekness — is conspicuous by its absence today. Everything is instant — right now, no waiting. The world is almost in a whirlwind of impatience.

But we are striving to rise above the world. Our concern is with learning the things of the Spirit. And one basic requirement for learning advanced spiritual things is patience — inexhaustible patience. Patience includes long-suffering, tolerance, mercy. It also expresses calm endurance under stress or adversity; it is the quiet waiting for solutions to problems, undergoing trials without complaint. Meek, patient willingness for God's will to be done, has such a softening effect on our emotions that we find God's thoughts unfolding within which lead to impressive demonstrations. Mrs. Eddy stresses humility when she writes, "Humility is lens and prism to the understanding of Mind-healing; it must be had to understand our textbook."

59

Temperance: The last quality listed in the Second Degree is temperance. It stands for self-restraint, self-control, moderation in action, thought and feeling.

In the First Degree, we find that for the most part, our thoughts and emotions control us; we do not have dominion over them. How often does our mind rehearse again and again events, conversations, conflicts and discord past and present, and we can't seem to control it? How often do we become angry, hurt, disappointed, fearful, depressed *involuntarily*? Do we act impulsively, doing thoughtless, unkind, selfish things which we later regret, things which cause us embarrassment and regret. Lack of control over our thoughts and feelings can cause us to act impulsively, unwisely, even unjustly. Some individuals have no control over the impulse to talk constantly. Nervousness, excitement, fear, insecurity, will cause the compulsive talker to go on and on rehearsing mortal mind as though he had no control over doing so.

When we seem mentally and emotionally out of control, unhandled animal magnetism is the cause. As long as we remain in the First Degree, our emotions appear to control us more often than not. But when we begin to demonstrate the Second Degree, we find that we can discipline our thoughts and emotions, and be in control of our mind.

As we progress spiritually, thought shifts from focusing on ourselves in a self-conscious, personal way, to focusing on God and His Science. Each day as we study and pray, as we discipline our mind and learn to control our emotions, we are practicing Christian Science; and in time this prayerful effort brings about the ability to control our thoughts and feelings to such a degree that we know when any foreign influence is intruding on our thinking and causing us to lose control of our mind.

This internal thought control is temperance or self-control. It is a great step beyond the chaotic and emotional mentality of the First Degree.

Such moderation in thought, word and deed, bestows refinement, graciousness, sensitivity, tactfulness. And isn't that Love individualized? Love lived in a natural and unassuming way?

In our day-to-day living, it is not necessary to rush about incessantly doing good for others, giving, giving, giving of ourselves. The spiritual love found in the Transitional Stage is one of stillness and peace. Our mental atmosphere offers to others a haven from the aggressiveness of animal magnetism, for it represents one who has achieved a mental atmosphere *void* of hate, fear, selfishness, aggressiveness, criticism, hostility, personal sense in all its forms. Instead, there is the gentle presence of kindness, patience, approval, understanding, forgiveness. Others will be drawn to the spiritual strength and peace we express as we demonstrate the Second Degree; and often it heals not only ourselves, but others as well.

Divine Love's Nearness Here and Now

We understand the Transitional Stage best if we study the synonym Love, for this stage is mainly one of feelings that have their origin in Love. Just as animal magnetism is the source and cause of mortal emotions, so Love is the source and cause of the Christly feelings of the Second Degree.

To understand Love is to realize our oneness with God as a present reality. For centuries the Christian world has been taught of a God who punishes man for sinning, of a God so distant from His creation and so remote from the individual man that a Christian must go through a priest or minister to reach God and have his prayers heard. Even in Christian Science, it is sometimes said, "God doesn't know anything about us."

But Christ Jesus said, "Your father knoweth what things ye have need of before you ask him." And Mrs. Eddy tells us that God and man are one as Principle and idea. In *Science and Health* she writes of "'God with us' — a divine influence ever present in human consciousness . . ." While it is true that God does not know

61

a mortal mind filled with sin, it is still a fact that however dark the mind may be, this divine influence is always with us. It is the indestructible link we have with God throughout eternity. Through this divine influence, God's thoughts reach us and gradually spiritualize consciousness.

As God is Love, this influence, speaking to our inner self, is pure love. Because we do know the difference between love and hate, we can begin to know God most clearly through spiritual love.

God's love is everything we want it to be. As the one Father-Mother God, Love is all-inclusive. God's love for us never falters, never changes, never withholds any good thing from us. It never afflicts or punishes. In the whole of the universe, there is not one destructive element, not one negative emotion. Love is pure, untainted by sensualism, human sentimentality and emotionalism. And so it remains a constant factor in governing man and the universe. Like the law of gravity, we live in it; we cannot go beyond it, or escape its governing force. We do not know what it is like to be apart from its presence and power.

The divine Principle, Love, is unspeakably kind, tender, gracious. Its presence is the warm, pure atmosphere of gentle stillness, inspiration, joy, happiness, bliss, and freedom. Love is infinite giving. Love cares. Love unfolds. It never forces. It gently creates and sustains each idea in an environment of beauty, harmony and perfection.

Love cares, yearns, longs to save us from wrong-doing. Love is patient, understanding, forgiving. In *Unity of Good*, Mrs. Eddy writes of our relationship with God, "Now this self-same God is our helper. He pities us. He has mercy upon us, and guides every event of our careers. He is near to them who adore Him. To understand Him, without a single taint of our mortal, finite sense of sin, sickness, or death, is to approach Him and become like Him."

The fact is, no matter how deep we may be in mortal mind, we are never totally estranged from God. The divine influence in consciousness is established and maintained by God, and cannot be

destroyed by animal magnetism. It may be temporarily buried by
mortal mind; but as we yield up our false beliefs and traits, we find
this inner voice intact in the heart of consciousness, where it waits
to speak to us.

The universe is benign — a holy place that has no harmful
or destructive element, no painful experience, no disease or death.
As God's expression, man lives in this divine creation, enveloped in
the spiritual love of God. Man's thoughts are permeated with kindness, gentleness, purity, spiritual goodness. He has no need to defy
the law of Love. He does not know how to hate, judge, condemn
or harm another. Man in God's likeness is so pure of love that he is
incapable of thinking an unkind, ungodlike thought. He never drives,
pushes, forces, wills, dominates, or controls. He reflects. He is
confident that God will meet his every need. This absolute trust
never fails to bring about a perfect manifestation of demand and
supply. He is never encumbered by too many possessions, nor lacking any good thing. The divine Father-Mother God never fails to
supply his every need. Each individual idea is independently dependent on God alone for all things. To the extent that we reflect
divine Love, we are that man.

Two words that best define Love are *power* and *relationships*. In the human sense, power usually means control over
others. It can be despotic or benign, but it is not true power. True
power is dominion over all evil. To the extent that we reflect the
qualities of the Second Degree, we draw close to God and He
draws close to us. In this closeness, we are given the spiritual
understanding and wisdom to be in control of our life. We have
dominion over beliefs and circumstances that we could not control
before. God's loving care manifests itself in healing and protection.
There are times when the greatest proof we have of God's loving
care, is His prevention of discord and adversity in our lives.

We also learn, as we demonstrate more love, that it affects
our relationships. As we live love, we draw to us those who are
loving, while those who are still in the First Degree gradually fade

63

out of our experience. As we progress, we learn that we do not have to endure hateful relationships. Each must work out his own salvation. We do not have to shoulder the burden of proving Christian Science to others, but rather we learn to live Christian Science so gently and so completely that our example will reach those ready for it.

As we understand and live love, we become increasingly conscious of our divine oneness with God; we live in the spiritual universe of His creating, and are blissfully happy living under His care and protection. We read in *Science and Health*, "Christians rejoice in secret beauty and bounty, hidden from the world, but known to God." Daily blessings unfold that can only be attributed to the divine Love knowing and providing for our every need.

Thus, we begin to actually *be* spiritual man, for the divine individuality of man begins to appear as a visible manifestation of spiritual love, governed, cared for, and protected from all evil by the Father.

Love Defined through the Synonyms

We can further expand upon the nature of Love by relating Love to the other six synonyms for God.

Love is Principle: Principle is *origin, cause, source; law, order, unity.* It also stands for *honesty, integrity and reliability.*

As divine Principle, Love is eternal, all-powerful, ever-present. We do not know what it is like to live outside of or apart from Love, because there is no "outside" to it. We may not sense the presence of Love, but Love is always present.

The divine Principle, Love, is defined as the origin or cause of all things; then the universe and man originate in divine Love. The laws governing and unifying the universe are warm, gentle, kind, and good. There is nothing discordant or threatening in them.

All ideas are unified in harmony and perfection, and all move together in expressing the orderly unfoldment of God's plan.

Love is also the measurement of spiritual integrity, reliability, honesty, or what we call "being principled." Jesus illustrated this divine Principle in his parable of the father's love for the prodigal son. The son took his inheritance and squandered it. The father let him go to learn a lesson the son evidently needed to learn; and when the son returned, he found the father's love for him as great as it had always been. And to the self-righteous son who stayed home, the father said, "Son, thou art ever with me, and all that I have is thine." This love — impartial, compassionate, forgiving, patient, generous — never changed, never faltered, and was never withheld.

According to the human concept of principle, the father would have been justified in disowning his wayward son. But divine Principle compelled him to love and forgive his son. This illustrates the difference between the human concept of principle and the divine Principle, Love.

The human concept of principle as honesty and integrity, can be cold, hard, rigid, unforgiving, unyielding, and uncompromising in its stand for what is known as the human standard of right and wrong. How often we hear the remark, "This is not right," or "That is not according to principle," or "They didn't keep their word or live up to their promise." But we are measuring people and events according to human morals and standards, according to our own sense of right and wrong; and we are disturbed because someone or something threatens or deprives us of some good.

The divine Principle, Love, includes integrity and honesty, but in the Second Degree this word *honesty* is mellowed by spiritual love. Mrs. Eddy appears to be telling us that the law of Love supersedes the humanly defined concept of principle, which may be another form of self-righteousness and unforgiveness. Again and again, she writes of the divine Principle, Love. The *divine* Principle is not a hard-line, self-righteous stand for what we think is

65

right or wrong. *The divine Principle is Love.* I urge you to think a long time about the difference between the two.

When we place the divine Principle, Love, first, and live the qualities of honesty and integrity as attributes of Love, our demonstration of love enables God to protect us from fraud, dishonesty, and deceit.

Love is Mind: The attributes of Mind are *intelligence, wisdom, understanding.* Love and Mind are an important combination in the study of Christian Science. The human intellect void of spiritual love, but well versed in the letter of Science, can be cold, hard, rigid, self-righteous. It is a darkened state of mind that mistakes intellectualism for spirituality. On the other hand, a heart filled with faith and goodness, loving, generous, forgiving, without an understanding of Christian Science, is often so naive and innocent that it is totally unprotected from animal magnetism.

But intelligence and wisdom permeated with spiritual love are the "light of the world." Divine intelligence, wisdom and love are a combination essential to the complete demonstration of Christian Science.

Divine Love is intelligent, wise, understanding. Love is always present and acting to spiritualize consciousness, rather than allowing us to perpetuate a comfortable material existence in the Adam-dream. Human love wants to pity and comfort another in his problems, and make things right humanly. Divine Love acts to awaken us, to purify consciousness, to reform the inner self. It forces us out of mental darkness into the light of spiritual understanding. In these spiritual lessons, we have divine Love blending with the wisdom and intelligence of Mind.

When the inner self is softened with love, the ideas of Mind unfold the deeper things of God. These ideas are so radical, so different from mortal intellect, that they completely reform the mind. Animal magnetism and matter become increasingly vague and illusionary, and God is revealed as the only cause or creator of all things real.

Love is Spirit: Spirit is *substance*. Substance is that which underlies all outward manifestations, the permanent cause of all phenomena. It is that which makes a thing what it is.

As Spirit, substance is Love, this destroys the belief in hard, cold, godless matter. The ultimate cause of the universe is not found in the cold, lifeless belief of material cause and law. All atomic structure is under the control of Love. All atomic action is the action of Love.

Love is a harmless power. It is warm, pure, good. Therefore in the whole of God's creation, there are no harmful laws or elements, no mindless causes or forces, and no negative thoughts or emotions. We are not encased in a material body, trapped in a mindless atomic universe, controlled by the unmerciful forces and laws of matter. The divine Principle, Love, is one with Spirit, substance. All that exists is governed by the spiritual law of Love. Regardless of what we may believe concerning matter and its laws, the fact still stands that Love alone shapes, forms and colors the visible manifestation of all things. Therefore all things are harmless because they are the expression of Love.

As we grow in our understanding of this sublime fact, the belief in matter slowly disappears, and with it go the negative traits and emotions that arise from the belief in matter. It does seem that we cannot understand the unreality of matter until we see substance as the manifestation of the divine Principle, Love. In Christian Science, we do not do away with the material universe and body. We translate atomic structure back into its spiritual forms by understanding the underlying cause of all phenomena to be Spirit. We cannot discern the spiritual universe when thought is hardened by the emotions of the First Degree. Only as we demonstrate the Second Degree, is the inner self enlightened enough to see through the veil of matter and discern God as the cause and creator of all things.

67

Love as Soul: Soul has many definitions. It is spiritual *ego, identity, individuality*; the spiritual senses of Soul are the opposite of the five physical senses. In the transformation from the First Degree to the Second, Love as Soul has a very special role. The spiritual ideas that unfold to us subjectively enter as a revelation in the heart of consciousness. Soul is the inner voice through which God's thoughts come to us. Through Soul comes the inspiration of divine ideas. When consciousness is darkened by mortal traits and beliefs, negative emotions silence our inner rapport with God. A mind hardened with selfishness and hatred, or paralyzed by fear, is impervious to the spiritual ideas that reform consciousness. But a mind softened with love is inspired with a flow of spiritual ideas.

Spiritual intuitions and ideas, unfolding within, are formed in and of Love. We begin reforming the inner self in the Second Degree as these ideas find receptivity in a mental atmosphere filled with love for them.

These ideas are our true identity or individuality. Reflecting Soul, they express the Soul-like qualities of beauty, loveliness, graciousness, spiritual intuition, sensitivity, gratitude, self-restraint, comeliness, humility — all related to divine Love. Love and Soul are inseparable. The spiritual intuitions that spiritualize consciousness unfold in a heart and mind that has learned to love, and eventually our true selfhood knows only the presence and power of those thoughts and feelings that reflect divine Love.

Love is Life: Life is *being*. Neither Life nor Love is passive or inert. Love must express itself as inexhaustible being, action, vitality. Mrs. Eddy writes, "Infinite progression is concrete being." Progressive life is Love expressing itself in ideas. Creation is dynamic, but it is never forced in its unfoldment. The creativity of God is void of stress, strain, struggle, drive, conflict or competition. Love as Life acts effortlessly, because there is nothing in reality to resist it. It is tender and gentle, strong and pure. All true being unfolds in Love; and man and the universe offer no resistance or obstruction to this unfoldment, because Love and its expression are one as cause and effect.

As we are increasingly aware of the kingdom of God within, we have no resistance to God's will operating in our life. As we give up false traits of the First Degree and demonstrate more love, we discover that we are never separated from God. He is as near as our thoughts, governing all the events and details of our life — when we let Him. It is the darkened thought of the First Degree that constructs a mortal life of discord and difficulties. As this degree lessens, the presence of God in our daily experience unfolds. The more we reflect Love, the better our life, for Love is Life.

Love is Truth: The word that best defines Truth is *reality*. In the search for Truth, the human mind has devised complex, seemingly profound and advanced metaphysical systems of ideas that are more or less an extension of present material views. These systems do not heal and regenerate mankind. They do not reveal Truth or reality. Truth remains unknown until we abandon our material personality, and demonstrate spiritual love. It is through a mind inspired by love that the structure, laws, nature, and qualities of reality unfold to us. Truth or spiritual knowledge, so profound and powerful, is incomprehensible to the darkened mortal mind. A demonstration of spiritual love precedes this advanced unfoldment of Truth that frees us of the mortal dream.

Again it is essential to see that Truth, this rocklike foundation of spiritual understanding, remains hidden or unknown to the mind that is hardened by mortal emotions and the error that we may assume to be truth. The so-called intelligence, the complex structure of human knowledge, that we presently think in, is not Truth. Truth is that understanding of God which enables us to do the works that Christ Jesus did. He had a form of intelligence that was absolute Truth — the Truth we are all seeking.

69

This brief review of the synonyms is meant to serve as an example of how Love can be better understood when it is related to the other six terms for God. Through your own unfoldment, you can expand on these ideas. Then when you think Love, it will have great depth and meaning to you. This understanding of Love will lay a strong foundation for demonstrating the Second Degree.

The Second Degree is very simple and straightforward. And yet to live it seems to be one of the most difficult achievements an individual can make. Even one who is greatly accomplished in the arts or sciences, or has perfected his talents, or is endowed with wealth, education, and position, or has the qualities of genius, brilliant intellect and creativity, may show forth little of the Second Degree. Yet it is the gateway to our escape from evil and our entrance into the kingdom of God. The First and Second Degrees provide a clear separation between the darkened mortal thought and the consciousness in which spiritual light is dawning. The Second Degree is an elementary Christ-consciousness, embodying the first appearance of our true selfhood in God's likeness.

However, the work of casting off the old and realizing the new, requires much more than recognizing the difference between the First and Second Degrees. Spiritualizing consciousness is the lifetime work of the consecrated metaphysician. It is possible because we have in Christian Science the metaphysical writings and the form of prayer that enable us to transform consciousness.

Chapter V

STUDY AND TREATMENT

*Draw nigh to God, and He will draw nigh
to you.*
JAMES

*Desire is prayer; and no loss can occur from
trusting God with our desires, that they may
be moulded and exalted before they take form
in words and deeds.*
MARY BAKER EDDY

It should seem a simple thing to reform the mind and emotions once we know the reasons for doing so. But this transformation proves to be difficult because animal magnetism resists its
own destruction.

It has become generally known that negative emotions are
the cause of mental and physical illness of every kind. Helping
others to overcome harmful emotions has posed a great problem to
psychiatrists, doctors, hypnotists, holistic practitioners, even spiritual healers. They have found that actually eliminating from consciousness the sickness-producing mental elements is the ultimate
challenge.

Doctors may cure through operations and drugs. Psychiatrists and other mental healers may help patients overcome emotional pain and trauma, and enable them to lead a normal existence.
But these cures take place in the First Degree. The person ex-
changes a suffering mental or physical condition for one termed a
more normal state of mind, but the mind remains very human, still
holding to its mortal personality. The struggle to bring change through

71

will-power or hypnosis, counseling, drugs or faith-healing, are human means. They do not transform the mind.

This even proves so in Christian Science when the one needing healing will not admit to any need to change his thinking, often blaming the problem on physical causes or malicious malpractice.

Healings that simply return the person to what he considers a normal existence, are no threat to animal magnetism, for the person is still convinced that evil is real and powerful.

Healing work in Christian Science is different. It is based upon the fact that evil is unreal, an illusion. The consecrated student is working to overcome the conviction that evil is real. This is basic to finding permanent healing. When we work from this standpoint and realize healing, we are working correctly. Healing frees the mind of some belief in animal magnetism's mesmeric hold.

We cannot find such freedom so long as we hold to the conviction that evil is real. Yet such a stand is in direct opposition to what the world holds as obvious fact, for evil does seem very real indeed. Thus Mrs. Eddy's declaration that evil is unreal came from a revelation that was truly incredible. When we consider the seeming power, enormity and aggressiveness of animal magnetism, we can never be grateful enough for her vision and courage in giving us a discovery that not only assures us of evil's nothingness, but gives us the metaphysics and form of prayer by which we can *prove* evil's unreality.

We prove the nothingness of animal magnetism each time our understanding of Truth is brought to bear upon a claim, and the claim is met. By proving evil's nothingness, we learn that animal magnetism is truly an illusion, or a myth.

However, in the First Degree, animal magnetism appears to be a power greater than God. It claims to control our thinking to such an extent that we cannot seem to escape its harmful influence. Through its hypnotic hold, it obstructs the unfoldment of spiritual ideas — unless we understand how to break its spell.

In Christian Science we learn how to handle evil and transcend mortal mind through *study* and *treatment*. The success of this work sets Christian Science apart from other healing methods.

Transforming Consciousness

When Christian Science is introduced into consciousness, we begin to transcend the mortal mentality and claim our dominion over evil. This is the beginning of evil's destruction. Animal magnetism resists this mental activity, and tries to prevent it from taking place. If we do not understand this resistance, we remain for the most part in the First Degree. We may realize healing of certain problems, but the Adam-dream is unchallenged and continues basically the same.

Our work in Christian Science is not to find ease and comfort in a good human life, but to spiritualize consciousness until we have dominion over all evil. We should begin to establish a state of mind so illumined with spiritual realities that we are lifted above the chemicalization taking place in the world around us.

It would help to give an example of this idea of transforming consciousness in Christian Science, so that we can visualize the goals before us. The mental atmosphere of the Dark Ages was filled with superstition and false theology — which was considered to be intelligence. Nowhere in the world did there exist a single book putting forth scientific information as we know it today. With the coming of the Renaissance, the early scientists began to give scientific law and order to the universe. As this new knowledge kept coming to light, it gradually transformed the minds of the civilized world until today we think in an entirely different mental state than those of three hundred years ago. And to the degree that we accept and use these scientific discoveries, we are blessed with a better life. We have *transcended* the mentality of the Dark Age by developing a scientific mind.

In centuries to come, the world will think in spiritual realities as naturally as we think in scientific knowledge. In our study of

Christian Science, we are discovering spiritual facts and developing a different state of mind, because we have a more advanced intelligence replacing false concepts presently considered to be intelligence or truth.

Like the natural sciences, Christian Science is a universal Science. It belongs to everyone. We can each do our own metaphysical work, handle our own problems, and demonstrate unlimited good in proportion to our understanding of God.

Study and Prayer

Our spiritual progress begins in earnest when we make a total commitment to the study of Christian Science with the purpose of learning to demonstrate it. It is one thing to know *about* Christian Science and to have absolute faith in it as the full revelation of Truth, but "faith without works is dead." We are still in the First Degree if we cannot intelligently demonstrate it. And so we must make it our business to understand it, and this is done through study and prayer.

Our first healings are usually efforts to overcome some extremely discordant problem — aggressive claims of sickness, disease, discord, lack, etc. When we do not have these challenges, we may study Christian Science in a rather detached way, for lack of a focal point or something specific to treat.

Whether we are humanly comfortable and coasting along, or trying to meet a claim that will not yield to our work, we can begin a better demonstration of Science by learning to obey the law of Love. We should try to determine how much of Christian Science we understand and demonstrate, and how much we accept on blind faith — taking care not to *assume* that we have more of the Spirit than we do.

We must go beyond a superficial use of Christian Science, in which we only handle the *effects* of sin — the discord and sickness that disturbs the so-called normal life. We must do more than

74

handle the effects of sin. We need to handle the sin itself. We
should examine the inner self to see how much unloving, selfish,
judgmental, critical, unforgiving thoughts and feelings we harbor
secretly, how much we express them towards others, how much
fear paralyzes our mind, and how much animal magnetism claims
of us in other ways. Through an honest analysis, we begin to
detect obvious errors or sins that we need to handle.

   Thus our work has a focal point. We can resist those
thoughts and emotions that violate the law of Love. These sins,
however, are the *effects* of animal magnetism. We can go one step
further and handle the final cause of mortal mind — *the solid conviction in the power and reality of evil*. When we handle this,
we strike at the very root of all sin, sickness, disease, and death.
Mrs. Eddy states in *Science and Health*, "Every mortal at some
period, here or hereafter, must grapple with and overcome the mortal belief in a power opposed to God."

   It is obvious that we cannot overcome animal magnetism
simply by analyzing it and theorizing about its nothingness. We
demonstrate our dominion over it by knowing about God. We must
understand both the nature of God and the nature of evil to escape
its hypnotic influence.

   Christian Science makes an absolute separation between
good and evil, Truth and error, Spirit and matter. It shows one to be
real, and the other to be unreal. It also gives us the metaphysical
writings and the form of prayer which enable us to leave the First
Degree for the Second.

   When we are in the First Degree, God seems very remote,
almost non-existent. Our prayers may then be supplications to Him
for help, but evil can seem so real and powerful that our prayers
appear to go unanswered.

   As we study Christian Science, we learn that God is as
close to us as our thoughts. We are one with Him now. And
through study and prayer, we gain the spiritual understanding that
brings this oneness to light. Our closeness to God is subjective.

75

We feel His nearness in the unfoldment of spiritual ideas; in the presence of love, inspiration, joy, peace and confidence; in the realization of Truth; in the transcending intelligence that reveals the spiritual nature of man and the universe as a present fact.

Study

We develop this inner rapport with God through the continuous study of Christian Science. Our study should include reading and pondering the best material available on Christian Science. First and foremost are the Bible and Mrs. Eddy's published writings. There are also many papers and books that explore the more advanced concepts set forth in the textbook. These are available through The Bookmark and other sources.

We cannot begin too soon using every opportunity to *read Christian Science.* Even if we do not understand what we are reading, we must read it. It is the only escape we have from the First Degree. Nothing put forth by mortal mind, however impressive or educational, will deliver us from evil. Only the mind that understands God, can counteract the mesmeric hold of animal magnetism, and escape the suffering route out of mortality.

Our study hours each day provide time and space in consciousness for the unfoldment of spiritual ideas. The purpose of our work is to gain some new insight daily into the allness of God and the nothingness of evil. The more secure we grow in our understanding of God as ever-present Love, the more we are convinced that evil is unreal, and the more we overcome fear, hatred and self-will. We naturally begin to embody the qualities of the Second Degree. Study alone is a form of prayer.

Our sincere desire to become more loving and enlightened, will cause the books and papers on Christian Science to be filled with inspiration. Such enlightenment will enable us to see our faults and correct them. Through study and prayer, we dissolve the hardened emotions within.

Animal Magnetism's Resistance to this Work

As we work against animal magnetism, we begin to understand its strong mesmeric nature, for we will feel its resistance to this work from the outset.

When the more advanced teachings of Christian Science are introduced into the mental atmosphere of a dedicated Scientist, it signifies the eventual end of evil's mesmeric hold on him. We begin to transcend the mortal mentality and claim our dominion over evil. This is the beginning of evil's destruction and so animal magnetism resists this mental activity and tries to prevent it from taking place. When you take up this work, animal magnetism will put you to sleep — a heavy sleep that is almost like a mesmeric trance. It will cause you to procrastinate. It will divert your mind to other things, cause it to wander, ruminate, plan, think about everything but the metaphysical work at hand. It will send interruptions. As we begin to challenge animal magnetism, we come to realize what a strong hold it seems to have on us. It is basically what we have been thinking in throughout our lifetime. As we take up our study, we find that evil is not passive or inert. It is aggressive, and we must be aggressive in our determination to be free of it. Mrs. Eddy once told a student, "Animal magnetism is powerless — but you must declare against it as though it had *all power*."

Because of this powerful mesmeric control, we cannot at this stage of our work ignore it as "nothing." We must learn to demonstrate our dominion over it. We do this by *resisting it* and learning to *control it* at every opportunity and doing so until we overcome it. Each time we resist it and demonstrate our control over it, we rid consciousness of some degree of mesmerism. We can do this because we have the truth about God with which to deny and destroy it. In this way, we learn to *control* evil and matter. As we learn to resist evil with Truth, we can feel the mesmerism weaken and fade away. Thus we learn that we can actually destroy animal magnetism's claim to be our thinking.

If we really want to find the kingdom of God within, we will not let animal magnetism keep us from an in-depth study of Christian Science. It is absolutely essential that you make as much time as possible for God, and you must not let evil prevent you from doing so. This thinking time is essential to entering the spiritual realm, and nothing should keep you from it.

Christian Science Treatment

If reading and pondering Christian Science were enough to renovate the inner self, many dedicated students of Christian Science would be much further along in their dominion over animal magnetism than they are. A study of the letter is absolutely essential to this work, and it does bring about healing and regeneration. But we are most successful in our demonstration of Science when we work with the treatment. This unique method of prayer is the secret to spiritualizing thought. *Indeed, the treatment is everything!*

Mrs. Eddy provided us with a means for praying effectively when she gave us the unique form of prayer — the prayer of affirmation and denial.

In this prayer, we take the initiative and argue *for* the allness of God and *against* the belief in evil and matter. We affirm the Truth and deny the error. That is why it is called the prayer of affirmation and denial.

Nothing is so effective in de-mesmerizing consciousness and freeing it of the claims of animal magnetism, than a strong and aggressive denial of a specific belief or trait, and the affirmation of the truth about God and man. All of our study and self-examination and the desire to spiritualize consciousness, is brought into focus and carried forth into healing results through this powerful and intelligent form of prayer. In the heart of prayer, you assert your right to be free of all belief in evil, and you argue — even *fight* — against the mesmerism seeming to be your thinking; and then you quietly but confidently affirm the truth about God and man, and identify with your affirmations by knowing you are that man. In doing this, you chemicalize consciousness and spiritualize it. It is essential that you identify with your metaphysical work.

The prayerful work of affirming the truth and denying the error was given in six footsteps by Mrs. Eddy to the early students. It is not a formula, but a basic outline of a prayer that is scientific and effective in proving evil's unreality and God's allness. The study of Christian Science, coupled with the treatment, is the most powerful form of intelligence on the earth today. It is the key to the kingdom within.

Simply stated, the treatment is as follows:

1) Begin by protecting the treatment. Silently declare that this is a Christian Science treatment; it is the Word of God, and the truth about God and man. It cannot be reversed or annulled by animal magnetism or malpractice. This part of the treatment is short, but your declaration helps to keep animal magnetism from claiming to invade your thoughts and reverse your work.

2) The second footstep affirms God through the synonyms — Spirit, Soul, Mind, Principle. Life, Truth, Love. Each synonym can be clearly defined through the attributes that apply most specifically to that synonym. Life is being; Truth is reality; Love is power and relationships; Mind is intelligence, wisdom and understanding; Spirit is substance; Soul is identity; Principle is law. The synonyms can also be related to each other. For example: Life is Mind; being is intelligence, wisdom, spiritual understanding. Life is Truth; joy, strength, vitality is the reality of being. Life is Love; real existence must be permeated with the warmth and power of spiritual love. Life is Spirit; true being is found in the substance of spiritual understanding. Life is Soul; being is comprised of the ideas or qualities that make up true identity. Life is Principle; being is governed by the divine laws of God, laws which cannot be denied or reversed.

Each synonym can be related to all the others, and as this work progresses, we come to understand the nature of God.

3) In the third footstep, relate man and the universe to the synonyms. In doing this we come to understand that they are spiritual, not material, in nature. They are the effect of a spiritual cause, and not the result of mindless matter.

The second and third footsteps are the affirmative part of treatment.

4) The fourth footstep involves the strong and aggressive denial of evil and its effects — mortal man and a material universe. In this footstep, you can deny matter through the synonyms: There is no matter in Life, and no life in matter; no matter in Truth, and no truth in matter; no matter in Mind, and no mind in matter; etc. You can deny all forms of fear, hatred, and selfishness. And lastly, you can deny the very existence of evil as a power or reality.

The fourth footstep is the denial part of treatment and is especially effective, for the truth is brought directly to bear on animal magnetism, and this will bring about a chemicalization that de-mesmerizes consciousness and reveals new insights into God and man.

5) In the fifth footstep, you can reaffirm the oneness of God and man, so that your work does not end on a negative note.

6) Then you can complete the treatment by once again protecting it, knowing it is the Word of God and cannot return to you void, but must accomplish its purpose.

I have explained the treatment in detail in my transcripts, *The Prayer of Affirmation and Denial,* and *Christian Science Treatment: The Prayer that Heals.*

The prayer of affirmation and denial is extremely effective. It is a prayer of action. We take the initiative and *argue for* the truth and *fight against* the claims of error in our own consciousness.

In the quiet hours of this metaphysical work we come to understand God better. We feel His nearness and hear within the spiritual ideas that reveal our oneness with the Father. We learn to destroy animal magnetism in all of its many guises. Through this work we gradually develop in consciousness a solid conviction that God is real and all-powerful, and that evil is powerless and unreal.

Treatment Essential

As we strive to demonstrate the law of Love, we find the treatment to be an indispensable part of this work. Neither the simple desire to change, nor the hours of study and quiet meditations on the truth, will dissolve deeply entrenched mortal traits within. Many traits seem so tenacious, so indelibly impressed upon our human nature, that we cannot overcome them through study alone. Determined efforts to erase them from consciousness through will-power prove of little worth. But they will yield when they are handled as animal magnetism in the treatment. We must handle them specifically, and do so with strength and persistence. The treatment enables the individual to fight against all forms of animal magnetism hidden within, and overcome them through his own prayerful work. It gives him power to govern his own life. He no longer has to depend on others for his freedom from all mortal claims. He can demonstrate his own way into the spiritual realm.

The treatment has been known since the early days of the Christian Science movement. It has been used to heal every claim of discord, sickness, disease, and limitation. As a rule it is used to meet mainly physical illness, extreme lack, grief, accidents, any claim of animal magnetism that disrupts what we consider to be normal health and daily routine.

But in demonstrating the law of Love, we can use treatment to change our present mental state of mind by treating false traits until they give way to spiritual love. We can repeatedly deny all forms of fear, selfishness, and hatred, and resist them until they fade away. And we can affirm as the truth about ourselves the qualities of Love — humility, honesty, affection, compassion, patience, forgiveness, gratitude, faith, hope, temperance.

Your daily metaphysical work will bring to the surface forms of animal magnetism hidden within and destroy them. And accompanying this chemicalization will be a revelation of truth and love that is new, replacing the false trait and transforming consciousness to some small degree. It is through the treatment that this mental renovation is most clearly felt and realized.

When such a reform takes place, we have a slightly new state of mind, and we think in it effortlessly. We naturally carry it forth into the world. We begin to *be* spiritual man.

Sin Not Permanent

Why is this transcending experience possible? Why should we expect to experience it? Because no false trait or sin is a permanent part of our being. It is unknown to God, it is unknown to man in His image. Therefore we can work from the basis that we can overcome all sin, and the belief in the reality of evil. Our progress in the beginning may be a little slow, for we have never before attempted to discipline and change our emotions. We are constantly changing our mind and disciplining it through education that enlightens and informs us intellectually. Now we are working to educate and discipline the emotions. This seems a great challenge, because we have never before tried to adapt to emotions that we are not used to. If we have a great fear of the future, we do not know what it is like to feel absolute trust in God to care for us always, and to be free of fear. If we are inclined to flare up over daily incidents that thwart us, we do not know how to deal with them patiently and turn to the one Mind in working them out. If we think we are in lack, we naturally see all that is considered a luxury as extravagance, rather than God's abundant provision for His idea, man.

Such traits seem so deeply ingrained in consciousness that they resist all human effort to reform them. We have lived in them for a lifetime and know nothing else. We think of them as normal.

Yet this mortal personality is not the real man in God's likeness. Therefore we can begin to change by accepting the fact that animal magnetism in the form of mortal traits can be overcome. As we work to rise above specific false traits, they will yield to our efforts. As they disappear, we are not left with a vacuum within. It might seem that as the mortal personality gives out, we become nothing. But quite the opposite! We begin to find our true selfhood in God's likeness. Fear becomes trust, faith, and confidence in God to care for us. Domination becomes humility, humanity, a gentle caring about others without any need to control them. Hatred and criticism yield to affection, compassion and understanding. Fretfulness, anxiety, sensitiveness yield to peace and rest.

Sometimes we can sense the change taking place when we are working metaphysically. But a false trait can be replaced by a Godlike quality so gently and gradually over months of study, that we can only recognize the change in ourselves by comparing our present state of mind with the one we had a year ago. And when we do, we see that we have made considerable progress Spiritward.

Through this prayerful work we learn to discern between those traits that harden the mind and those that soften it and make it receptive to God's thoughts. This work enables us to obey the law of Love, because it establishes a foundation of divine intelligence and love within. We graduate beyond mortal emotions into impartial, universal love.

We cannot strive enough to demonstrate love in our metaphysical work, because there comes what I call "the moment of truth" — when we must live spiritual love in the world.

Chapter VI

THE TESTING TIME

He that loseth his life for my sake shall find it.
CHRIST JESUS

Simply asking that we may love God will never make us love Him; but the longing to be better and holier, expressed in daily watchfulness and striving to assimilate more of the divine character, will mould and fashion us anew, until we awake in His likeness.
MARY BAKER EDDY

As you study and pray, yearning to know God better, you should come to feel the peaceful, inspiring, healing presence of God in this quiet time alone with Him. But there comes that time each day when you must leave your books and quiet meditation, and go forth to cope with the world — your close personal life with family and friends, and the outside world of acquaintances and strangers.

It is not hard to remain loving with those who are thoughtful and kind. But there inevitably arise those relationships and occasions when you are put to the test. You face that moment of truth when you must live the law of Love under stressful circumstances.

Someone is rude, inconsiderate, angry, insulting. He has a short temper and flares up at you. There is a conflict of opinion. You feel you have been used, misunderstood, unjustly criticized or accused, victimized by another's deceit or dishonesty. Someone doesn't keep his appointment, or he is late, or he does not carry out his promise to do something. A lack of integrity or care by another causes plans to go wrong. Mechanical things break down; your plane is late; you have to wait for an appointment; your order didn't arrive on time.

In these moments you are put to the test to *live* the law of Love. How do you react to the unloving treatment of others and the stress of circumstances? Do you *remain* kind, patient, understanding, and forgiving when the other person does not seem to deserve it? Do you continue to be loving when he does not respond to your kindness? Are you able to forgive him to such a degree that you do not think or feel unkindly towards him?

From the human standpoint you may be well within your rights to retaliate over the unloving, thoughtless, even hateful, treatment of others, to complain and criticize. But if you choose *not* to, you are returning love for hate, and learning to control your emotions. *It takes unbelievable strength to remain true to the law of love during such moments of trial!* If you believe that spiritual love is weak and effeminate, try living it in the world today, all the time with everyone, everywhere. Do try it!

Unfaltering love comes from strength, not weakness. It is built on moral and spiritual righteousness. We do not compromise with error or condone it. We stand for all that is right, but we stand lovingly! patiently! We forgive and forget!

It is most essential that we be *strong* in love. Spiritual love is not an over-developed state of human sentimentality. We are not to be doormats for others to walk over, use, abuse, or dominate. We can stand for that which is right in our most Godlike sense of justice and integrity, but we can do so kindly, patiently, courageously, and lovingly. This is *strong love*. And this way of handling animal magnetism will bring a victory over evil. In being strong in love, we never hurt persons, but we exercise dominion over the evil trying to handle everyone involved. We learn to be long-suffering, understanding of the other person's problems and viewpoints, and to be compassionate and forgiving of his human faults and failings.

To do this, how essential it is to understand that our good comes from God. If we have demonstrated all that we have, it can never be threatened or taken from us. We must see through the mortal picture being presented, and know that the individual who is wronging us is nevertheless the son of God. Then we can separate the animal magnetism handling the situation from all persons, impersonalize it, and make nothing of it. This keeps us from reacting to error that seems to come from others.

When the situation is especially trying, we may find it hard not to react to the malpractice, injustice, and hatred confronting us. When this happens, we need to withdraw and work metaphysically over the situation until it becomes unreal to us, and we are no longer emotional over it. As we persist in this, we discipline our emotions to be always loving. We then find it impossible to be unloving to anyone at any time for any reason.

The persistent effort to be loving *is* our practice. We are practicing Christian Science, just as one practices the multiplication tables or the musical scales in order to do them perfectly. When we meet a challenge with love, this is our daily exercise in loving. We often must be the *first to love*. When another gives us an impatient word or is unkind in some way, we can answer with kindness, patience and understanding. Often this will completely change the tone of a situation. If he thinks we are angry with him, we need to say or do something to let him know we are not. In this way we love first, and can often turn an unpleasant situation into a very good one.

By practicing spiritual love daily on everyone, it becomes very natural to be loving. We learn to be sensitive to unloving situations that are developing, and prevent them from taking place. We encounter an experience that would have, in the past, made us react emotionally. But we are now able to react only with love and forgiveness. Gradually through practicing love, we find we are *incapable* of hate or anger or impatience.

Probably the greatest cause of emotional distress is with family and friends — those we care the most about. Animal magnetism can seem most aggressive and challenging when it tries to attack us through those closest to us. Such relationships may confront us again and again through a selfishness and hatred and ingratitude that are a continuing part of our life. The solution may not be to dissolve the relationship, but to stay with it until we are able to remain absolutely unintimidated by the unloving words and acts of another. When we gain our dominion over error in this way, animal magnetism can no longer control us through such relationships.

One of the first and greatest lessons I had in learning the law of Love was with a close relative of many years ago. This woman was basically good, and she yearned to be loved and respected. But she had such a harsh, critical, almost hateful attitude towards others that I found it extremely difficult to be with her. Yet periodically I could not avoid her company for several weeks at a time. It was plain that she did not like me. I was as loving to her as I could be, but she didn't change in her attitude towards me. My patience and kindness did prevent ugly confrontations, simply because I would not argue with her. Once in talking this over with another Christian Scientist, he said, "Well, she may never change, but love her anyway." And so I did. And she did not change.

Once I was with her for several weeks in which I was extremely loving and kind, for I felt a great sense of compassion for her. It made no difference. She seemed so difficult, I could not help being disturbed by her dislike for me. After she left, I prayed again to know what to do about this. The answer came, "Cease to care."

This seemed a strange answer, but a possible solution to the problem. I realized that I was taking personally her antagonism and making a reality of it. Whereas I needed to impersonalize it, and see it all as animal magnetism, and be unmoved or undisturbed by it. I did manage to do this. It was not easy, but I stopped reacting to her critical, unkind treatment. I remained kind, loving, considerate, regardless of what she said or did, but I no longer took personally her criticism and hostility, for I realized that she was like this with everyone. I became unaffected by anything she said or did, and continued to be as kind to her as she would permit me to be. This didn't change her either. She remained the same until the end of the relationship. But I counted this experience as one of the greatest lessons I had ever had in learning to obey the law of Love, for I had learned to remain unmoved by the animal magnetism in another, even when it was directed towards me. When I no longer took her treatment personally I began to overcome personal sense. Over the years this has enabled me impersonalize animal magnetism in many similar experiences.

Difficult relationships are like catalysts. They bring to the surface forms of animal magnetism latent in us. These negative emotions lie dormant when things are pleasant. It is only when difficult, challenging situations confront us and we react with unloving emotions, that we realize how much animal magnetism still claims of us. At such times, we find self-justification, self-righteousness, self-pity, hatred, resentment, anger, revenge — many hidden mortal emotions rushing to the surface and handling us involuntarily. Until these false traits are agitated by a difficult experience and we recognize them in ourselves, they remain unhandled and can at any time cause us mental and physical suffering. *And whether they are latent or active in consciousness, they darken and harden the mind, and prevent the full unfoldment of truth from taking place.*

To demonstrate control over our reactions to the unloving words and deeds of others, is the challenge of the moment. From the small, thoughtless criticisms and put-downs to the on-going acts of open hostility, emulation, or domination — these can be viewed as our daily practice in learning the law of Love. They force us to a higher demonstration of love than we would make without these lessons. We grow strong in love when we can separate the error from the individual and stand unintimidated or unmoved by it.

In addition to the challenge of reacting to others, we have the responsibility for our own words and deeds. How careful we must be not to initiate anything unloving ourselves. To actually obey the law of Love in our inner self, in the secret thoughts and feelings underlying all that we say and do — this is the ultimate challenge. *No one knows what we are thinking!* How cleverly we can hide what we are really feeling when we want to. But this duplicity of mind is not permitted if we are to obey the law of Love.

Obedience to this law begins in the inmost thoughts, and it takes unrelieved self-discipline and great strength to obey this law in the very heart of our being — where there is no one to answer to but ourselves. Here in the hidden recesses of the heart and mind, we must sift our thoughts, reform our inner self in God's likeness, and retain only those elements that relate to divine Love. We *can* control how we think and feel. We *can* leave *un-thought, un-said and un-done* those things that are not loving. And in this way, we cultivate spiritual love until we think in it naturally, effortlessly. Then we cannot say or do anything unloving, because we never think anything unloving.

When we are in the First Degree, we seem sometimes to be under the control of what could be called *involuntary* anger or hurt feelings or fear. We can't seem to help feeling these emotions. We seem to have no control over them. Think what it would be like to be under the control of *involuntary* kindness and forgiveness and patience, of being incapable of feeling anything but love!

The argument comes, when this sermon on Love is preached, that there are instances when such love is not practical, that we should defend ourselves, that we must not let others take advantage of us, that we have our rights, and that there are times when such love is not always possible.

Humanly such arguments may be right, but you need to ask yourself what you want of Christian Science. If you want to remain in the "faith" stage — wherein you have great faith in it, but little understanding of it, then you may find that a total commitment to the law of Love is not practical at this time. But if you are in earnest about understanding and demonstrating Christian Science to its fullest, then obedience to the law of Love is a major step towards doing so. Love softens the mind and heart, and prepares you to receive that truth which is "hidden in sacred secrecy from the visible world."

If it is your goal to understand what Mrs. Eddy has given us, you will not be too concerned over what others are thinking and doing. You have one purpose in your work — *to prove yourself to God by obeying the law of Love.* In obeying this law, you are prepared to demonstrate the Third Degree. Consider this carefully, for it puts everything into perspective. You have God first. Christ Jesus said, "Seek ye first the kingdom of God, and his righteousness, and all these things shall be added unto you." We do this through demonstrating the law of Love.

Actually, we are surrendering the human for the divine. We are rising above being concerned over what mortal mind is thinking, over the need to please others, and learning to please God.

Chapter VII

THE HEALING RESULTS OF THIS WORK

Obey my voice, and I will be your God, and ye
shall be my people: and walk ye in all the
ways that I have commanded you, that it will
be well unto you.

JEREMIAH

Between the centripetal and centrifugal men-
tal forces of material and spiritual gravita-
tions, we go into or we go out of materialism
or sin, and choose our course and its results.
Which then shall be our choice, — the sinful,
material, and perishable, or the spiritual, joy-
giving, and eternal?

MARY BAKER EDDY

An effort to live the law of Love is known to God. It is
comforting to learn that God is as close to us as our thoughts, and
that we are not alone in this work of transcending mortal mind. As
we leave behind mortal traits and beliefs, spiritual enlightenment,
intuitions and inspiration fill the void. There appear in consciousness insights into Christian Science that illumine thought with inspiration and spiritual understanding. Thus we "emerge gently"
into the Second Degree. The wonder of this transcending experience is the effect it has on our life here and now.

It is a spiritual law that our thoughts govern our experience. Mortal thoughts produce a mortal existence. If we do not
understand Christian Science, our present life is primarily mortal
thought objectified. A dark, limited, material mind projects a life

91

like itself. Even when a mind is humanly good, it is not exempt from the suffering that the mortal dream produces, for it continues to embody the conviction in the reality of evil and matter.

We find however that as we demonstrate the Second Degree, we begin to exercise control over our life because we are learning to control our thinking. Through study and prayer, we demesmerize consciousness and demonstrate a foundation of spiritual understanding, which in turn manifests itself in ever-increasing good in our experience. Considering the loss of control over his life that the average individual is experiencing today, we begin to appreciate this power to demonstrate spiritual control that lies latent in Christian Science.

This control is wholly *subjective*. It comes through scientific prayer and demonstration. As we discern some new idea that adds to our basic understanding that God is all and evil is nothing, this changes how we think. As these ideas multiply, they spiritualize consciousness. Then they *must* manifest themselves in a better human experience. The change unfolds subjectively, before it appears outwardly.

Christian Science treatment is a prayer of action. In our treatment, we detect and deny the traits and beliefs that violate the law of Love. We free consciousness of the conviction that evil is real and has power. Thus we control and eliminate the negative thoughts and feelings that create a disturbed and fearful state of mind. Thus we prevent them from causing discord and disease in our experience.

Through the prayer of affirmation and denial, we learn to handle every mortal belief that suggests itself to us. We *refuse* to become angry, fearful, disturbed, unhappy over discordant events and circumstances. We detect and cast out beliefs and traits that seem an established part of consciousness. We constantly deny the power and reality of evil and matter.

Then we consciously cultivate the qualities of the Second Degree, and make every effort to live the law of Love. We discipline our thoughts and feelings to conform to the Christ-conscious-ness, and use our God-given ability to control what enters our mind and what goes on in it. This truth, active in thought, chemicalizes and changes our mortal nature. Into this warm, gentle, receptive mind, softened by spiritual love, God's ideas unfold as our own thoughts — inspiring ideas, creative ideas, intelligent ideas, practi-cal ideas. We learn to exercise the same "might and ability to subdue material conditions" that Christ Jesus had. Thought shifts from the insecure, ever-changing beliefs and emotions of animal magnetism to the stable foundation of spiritual understanding. Ven-turing ever deeper into the spiritual dimension, we come under God's control. Conviction in the reality of God, good, gradually over-comes conviction in the reality of evil. We transcend the normal human life for a life controlled by divine Love.

Each time we read and treat and practice spiritual love, we enlarge upon, establish, and reinforce our conviction in the pres-ence and power of God to govern our life, to protect and heal us, to supply our every need. This spiritualized thought reflecting divine Love, becomes a transparency for the power of God to control harmoniously our entire experience.

As we grow spiritually, we begin to lose our fear and belief in evil. We reform and purify consciousness. Then in accordance with the law that our thought creates our experience, this improved state of mind *must* move forth and be objectified in a better life. No form of animal magnetism can prevent this law from taking effect when we have demonstrated the good that is moving forth into visible manifestation.

As we emerge into the Second Degree, the spiritual love we live protects us from malicious mental malpractice, brings us health and longevity, and blesses our relationships, the place we live, our supply and daily experiences.

Protecting the mind from malicious mental malpractice: While we need to handle the animal magnetism originating within consciousness, we also must learn to shut out the aggressive mental suggestions coming from outside sources. Daily study and treatment enable us to discern the difference between the mesmeric suggestions of animal magnetism coming from outside sources and the ideas unfolding from Mind. By shutting out the one and cultivating the other, we learn to control what we accept into consciousness. In our daily work, we learn to deny the power and reality of evil. We do not allow the mesmeric lies of evil to enter consciousness. Since they cannot force us to accept them, thought is protected from their harmful influence.

If we *refuse* to let the aggressive mental suggestions of sickness, disease, disaster, accidents, lack and crime into consciousness; if we *refuse* to rehearse over and over every kind of discord and catastrophe, we control thought, and rule these beliefs out of our experience. In so doing, we prevent them from taking place.

The flood of evil suggestions coming for acceptance is overwhelming — all presenting evil as real, an ever-present threat to our health and well-being. These lies poured into consciousness, manifest themselves tangibly in every kind of discord. But as we see through the unreality of evil, we do not accept or react to these lies, and therefore they cannot manifest themselves in our experience.

Health and Longevity: Each day we should do specific work to counteract the belief in disease, age, and death. But we also find that handling false traits is absolutely essential to overcoming disease and old age, for false traits are the main cause of these beliefs. As we gain dominion over the belief in evil and matter, we lose the traits and beliefs that produce sickness, disease and age. Whereas the emotionalism of the First Degree may cause illness of every kind, the spiritual love of the Second Degree brings with it consistent health and well-being.

When we overcome mortal traits, we counteract the cause of age. Too often with the belief of failing eyesight, loss of memory, and other claims of old age, Scientists treat the physical problem and handle age. They do not realize that these claims are actually the *effects* of a chronic disobedience to the law of Love. The *habit* of hating, fearing, being consumed with the emotions of self-will and personal sense — these are the *cause* of disease and age. The physical problem claims to be incurable because the emotional habit underlying them is so ingrained that the individual apparently cannot or will not change. He does not understand that the basic cause of all physical claims is mental and emotional, and so he believes the claim is stubborn or incurable. In Christian Science, there is no incurable disease. If a physical problem does not yield, it is because the person cannot or does not want the demanding work of understanding God and obeying the law of Love. As we enter the Second Degree, we leave behind the most aggressive causes of old age. It is far better to *prevent* age than to try to overcome it once it is upon us. The most effective way to do this is to work out of the First Degree with its destructive emotional traits, and into the Second Degree with its spiritual elements that heal and prevent sickness, disease, and age. Thus we begin to experience life that is natural to man in God's likeness.

Relationships: Before we begin to study Christian Science, we are in the First Degree. We associate with minds like our own. Those around us are mortal, just as we are mortal in our thinking. It could be said that we live in a sea of mortal thoughts and emotions objectifying collectively a sensual, materialistic, discordant, sickly mortal life. Because of our spiritual interests, we may yearn to escape depressing, negative, difficult relationships.

As we demonstrate more and more of the Second Degree, our spirituality transforms consciousness, and we become *different* from those in the First Degree. We press on into that advanced intelligence that gives us dominion over mortal mind. Our emotional attraction and attachment to discord and materialism lessen and even disappear.

95

As we outgrow the First Degree, we leave behind the chaos and confusion, self-will, hatred and fear, the materialism, sensualism, and ignorance — all so unlike the spiritual love of the Second Degree. We find that we have less and less in common with the mortal scene. In her *Message to The Mother Church for 1902*, Mrs. Eddy writes of this experience, "O glorious hope! there remaineth a rest for the righteous, a rest in Christ, a peace in Love. The thought of it stills complaint; the heaving surf of life's troubled sea foams itself away, and underneath is a deep-settled calm."

As we advance into the Second Degree, our thoughts become increasingly spiritualized. This naturally separates us from the materialistic mentality that absorbs the worldly scene and lives by its standards. There is a great gulf between the materially darkened mind and the spiritually enlightened one — a gulf that daily widens as they move in opposite directions. We are "hid with Christ in God."

We find in our spiritual progress that we outgrow old thought-habits, opinions, beliefs, interests, and other things that seemed important and necessary to our former way of thinking. We leave behind outgrown vocations, pastimes, organizations, and relationships with whom we have less and less in common. We may feel that something is wrong as we leave the old for the new, but as the old drifts away and the new unfolds, this is again the law of Love operating to purify our lives and bring us out of the material world into the world of Spirit.

The one word that best describes this loss of earth-weights is *freedom*. The mental and emotional freedom, the lightness, the quiet peace and happiness that come with this release from mortal mind is truly summed up in our Leader's words, "Loss is gain."

Place: The more we reflect spiritual love, the happier the place where we live and work. So often an individual will move from one home to another, from one job to another, hoping to find a better life. But the new place becomes exactly like the old place because his thinking has not changed. He takes the same mind with him wherever he goes, and so he objectifies the same kind of life wherever he lives.

On the other hand, as we understand and express spiritual love, this work will lift us out of a place that is incompatible with our progressive thinking. It would not be in accord with the divine Principle, Love, for us to have to remain in a place we have outgrown. God does not require us to live on in a threatening, materialistic, abusive, or limited place, once we have risen above such a mental atmosphere. As we progress spiritually, we leave behind confining, discordant circumstances and places, and move into a better environment.

As we demonstrate spiritual love, our place or environment comes to express more and more safety, peace, affluence, beauty, purity and refinement — it has a quiet, gentle, God-like atmosphere where the qualities of Love are lived daily. There is a great happiness in being in a place God has prepared for us.

Daily Life: We begin to realize how close, how intimately involved, God is with His universe and man as we experience His care, provision, and protection in our day-to-day living.

When the inner self softens with spiritual love, we feel God's closeness and control in every way. He reminds us of things we should remember; leads us to lost articles; prevents our doing things that would bring about catastrophes, difficulties, embarrassment; opens the way to be on time; replaces indecision, uncertainty, impulsive and unwise words and deeds with spiritual intuitions that are always right; provides for unforeseen needs; cares for us in ways that relieve stress, frustration, indecision, hurry and worry. So often there are the many little aggravations that do *not* happen to us that prove God's nearness, His untiring care.

As we enter the Second Degree, the focus of our attention shifts from habits and pastimes that were once so all-absorbing to more spiritual activities and different associations. Time-consuming causes and organizations seem less and less important.

Again the key word in all of this change is *freedom.* Freedom from what? The many earth-weights that we are burdened with because we do not know how to escape them. Mortal mind would make us feel guilty if we do not support humanly good organizations, give generously of our time and money to many of its deserving causes, and conform to the world. But always remember that we are involved in the ultimate Cause — the work of spiritualizing world consciousness. Each time we pray, heal, and prove Christian Science to be the promised Comforter, we are giving our all to help humanity. This prayerful work is the hope of the world. It is little wonder that animal magnetism tries in every way to stop our doing it.

Through our dedication to Christian Science, we learn that we are not being disobedient to God by leaving behind the many demands and attractions of the world in order to make time and space in consciousness for God's thoughts to reach us. Each time our spiritual progress severs some link with mortal mind, the result is freedom from some earth-weight that we are ready to give up. This freedom, promised by the Master Metaphysician, is wonderfully light and restful.

Supply: The Second Degree unfolds the means for demonstrating supply more abundantly. True supply comes through spiritual resources — the infinite reservoir of ideas found in Mind. These ideas are practical, intelligent, creative, as well as spiritual. Having their origin in Mind, they are destined to fulfill their purpose when we discern them. As we spiritualize consciousness, we turn to God for those ideas that enable us to demonstrate supply.

An abundant life is the natural state of man. Christ Jesus said, "I come that they might have life, and that they might have it more abundantly." And Mrs. Eddy explained the way to an abundant life when she wrote in *Miscellaneous Writings*, "God gives you His spiritual ideas, and in turn, they give you daily supplies. . . and if you wait, never doubting, you will have all you need every moment." Through the divine influence within our own conscious-ness, we have God's thoughts coming to us in the form of ideas. And because Mind is infinite, we have within an inexhaustible source of supply unfolding within. Thus the source of true supply is through the discernment of God's ideas.

In order to discern these ideas, we must be able to hear God's voice. He must be able to reach us. When the mind is hardened with mortal emotions and beliefs, we cannot hear His voice; and so we continue to live in lack and limitation. But as thought softens, and self-will, fear, and hatred are replaced by the elements of the Second Degree, we can discern God's thoughts taking form in ideas or intuitions that meet our needs. These ideas are the source of true supply. Money, possessions, wealth, can be lost or depleted. But when we depend upon God's thoughts to meet every need, our supply is inexhaustible. Our life should not be one of frugality, stringency, and poverty, but one of unfolding ideas that bring an abundance of good to us.

The spiritual source of supply is demonstrated by the mind that listens from within, trusts the ideas that God unfolds, and acts on them or uses them. This requires great faith in God to care for us. Mrs. Eddy writes of "never doubting." Christ Jesus said, "Your father knoweth what things ye have need of, before ye ask him." God's care is immediate. Even before we are aware of the need, He has anticipated it and already provided the need and the chan-nels necessary for its manifestation.

For this reason, we can go forward into the Second Degree without fearing that we are leaving behind the traits that enable us to deal with the world and make a living in the market place. As we actually live the law of Love, we find that this does not deprive us of success in the world, but rather it so enhances our abilities and enlarges upon our talents that we are able to demon-strate our supply in even greater abundance.

Conclusion

As we learn to love, and continue our struggle to understand the unreality of matter and evil, *we come to be an early manifestation of spiritual man.* We have the "might and ability to subdue material conditions." This spiritual understanding is a mighty protection from the evil that is so aggressive in the world today.

As we demonstrate our dominion over evil, we feel God's presence caring for us in both the large affairs and the small details of our life. We find our metaphysical work heals with great power.

There is also an unseen, undetected power in this work that both comforts and encourages those of us who are concerned over the suffering of humanity. The work you do each day for yourself radiates out into world consciousness, chemicalizes the error in it, brings the error to the surface, and begins the healing process. Surely much of the chemicalization going on in the world today is the result of the years of prayerful work done in Christian Science — all of it taking place not only to heal individual problems, but to heal world conditions as well.

Slowly as we grow in love and spiritual understanding, we become conscious of this spiritual dimension underlying and permeating the universe as a concrete reality. It is the presence of a thinking, knowing Mind governing all. To the degree that man — individually and collectively — lives in this divine intelligence and love, he realizes the kingdom of God within. As this dimension comes to light, it promises to bring infinite good to humanity.

Surely three hundred years ago no one could have foreseen the scientific world that is now an accomplished fact. The universal emergence into the scientific dimension has enlightened and blessed mankind. It has given him control over his physical environment.

The universal emergence into the spiritual dimension is a forthcoming event that will enable man to control his mental environment. As the kingdom of God unfolds throughout the world, we will see the coming of the millennium. Of this blessed event, Mrs. Eddy writes in *Science and Health*: "One infinite God, good, unifies men and nations; constitutes the brotherhood of man; ends wars; fulfills the Scripture, 'Love thy neighbor as thyself;' annihilates pagan and Christian idolatry, — whatever is wrong in social, civil, criminal, political, and religious codes; equalizes the sexes; annuls the curse on man, and leaves nothing that can sin, suffer, be punished or destroyed."

To hasten the coming of the spiritual age, we can ask ourselves in all that we think and say and do: "Is it in accord with the law of Love?"

For further information regarding Christian Science:
Write: The Bookmark
Post Office Box 801143
Santa Clarita, CA 91380
Call: 1-800-220-7767
Visit our website: www. thebookmark.com